# Maturing a Christian Conscience

# MATURING A CHRISTIAN CONSCIENCE

## JOHN CARMODY

THE UPPER ROOM
Nashville, Tennessee

Cover Design: Harriette Bateman
Cover Transparency: James C. Sternberg
Book Design: B. J. Osborne
First Printing: June, 1985 (3)
Library of Congress Catalog Card Number: 84-052232
ISBN 0-8358-0510-7

Printed in the United States of America

*For Bill Davenport*

# CONTENTS

# PREFACE

This book is an effort to help Christians who want to know how their consciences, their moral intelligences, might mature. Its bent is to consider Christian conscience the place where God would meet us for transforming prayer. From the reflections and discernments that prayer, our loving communion with God, develops come our best appreciations of what we should be trying to do at work, in our family lives, around the neighborhood, in secular or church politics. It is the love poured forth in our hearts by the Holy Spirit that makes us ethical as we want to be, good and useful to others. It is consciences formed by this love, so open to the Spirit that the Spirit makes the groaning prayer in their depths, that find the grit to prophesy and give witness. Thus while the book gives cases and deals in principles, it refuses to see Christian ethics as anything but a species of Christian spirituality. Specialized knowledge can be necessary in particular areas, but even there ripe fruit will only come from the grace of the divine love beating strongly in the heart.

My thanks to Janice Grana and Rueben Job for encouragement and advice; to my wife Denise for cheery irreverences that kept things in perspective; and to Karla Kraft for top-notch manuscript preparation.

# 1.

# INTRODUCTION

## *The Notion of Conscience*

Once there was a young man whose family ran a meat-market. He was the last of many brothers and sisters, the bright-eyed and bushy-tailed favorite. The family's business was doing well, expanding and adding new stores, so everyone expected the young man to make his career in the meat business. That was fine with him. He liked dealing with people, staying on top of inventories, bringing home a fat paycheck. Still, he was an idealistic young man, concerned to do what was right, anxious to make a contribution and help other people. Thus it was a heavy blow for him to discover that his older brothers were shady tradesmen who gave their customers light weights and paid their employees low wages. When he confronted them with these discoveries, they laughed and told him to grow up. How did he think the business had prospered? What did he think other meat-markets did?

Walking the streets at night, turning over his brothers' responses, the young man realized that he didn't care what other meat-markets did. His brothers' way of doing business was wrong, something that made him feel tainted. The prospect of a career alongside them was depressing, so he began to think of alternatives. He had always enjoyed school. Maybe he ought to go to college, expand his horizons. He could study economics, broaden his background in case he wanted to return to business. He could take courses in psychology, literature, history, and other things that might be interesting. So he went to college, got involved in economics, and eventually struck out on a career in educational administration. By the end of his career he was nationally prominent as a spokesman for liberal education. His life, and the lives of hundreds of students, were markedly different because of pangs of conscience he once suffered.

On occasion we speak of a person suffering *scruples*. The image behind this word is of a pebble lodged in one's shoe. It is sharp, irritating, something one must deal with before being able to progress comfortably. The young man's unease with his brothers' business practices amounted to scruples of conscience. When he took stock, reflected on what this sharp dealing portended for his future, he found pain and irritation. The dishonesties in which he was likely to become involved rubbed him the wrong way, blocked his path. He had to get this thing removed, resolved, off his mind. Until he did he would have no peace, his joy would be clouded over. When he made the decision to leave the family business, his spirits rose. His way was again clear, he needn't limp and feel torn.

Consider another, more famous young man:

And behold, one came up to him, saying, "Teacher, what good deed must I do, to have eternal life?" And he said to him, "Why do you ask me about what is good? One there is who is good. If you would enter life, keep the commandments." He said to him, "Which?" And Jesus said, "You shall not kill, You shall not commit adultery, You shall not steal, You shall not bear false witness, Honor your father and mother, and, You shall love your neighbor as yourself." The young man said to him, "All these I have observed; what do I still lack?" Jesus said to him, "If you would be perfect, go, sell what you possess and give to the poor, and you will have treasure in heaven; and come, follow me." When the young man heard this he went away sorrowful; for he had great possessions.

—Matthew 19:16–22

This young man also has a question of conscience. He has been bothered about how he has been spending his life, what he has been making of himself. So he goes to the rabbi his friends are talking about and asks him for guidance. The rabbi gives him traditional enough advice, things he's mastered for some time. In Mark's version of the story (10:21), Jesus loves the young man for his goodness, seeing him as a candidate for higher things, extraordinary service in the Kingdom. But the young man is not ready to bear Jesus' further counsel, cannot yet hear a call to full freedom and service. Saddened by the hold that riches have on him, Jesus uses the young man's bondage to warn the disciples about the seductions of money. It may be, though, that as the young man matured, Jesus' counsel lingered at the back of his mind. Testing the satisfactions that his wealth brought, comparing what they did to his spirit with what Jesus' example of freedom had done, he may one day have concluded that the rabbi was right. Putting aside his possessions, he may have set off to answer the call he could now hear, feed his hunger for a full service of God.

These two examples are meant to suggest the functions and significance of the faculty that we call *conscience*. Because we human beings can reflect and be somewhat responsible for our actions, we are aware in ways that subhuman creatures are not. The general name for this awareness is *consciousness* (or *reflective consciousness*). When our awareness focuses on moral matters—questions of choice, ethics, values—we speak of *conscience*. Conscience, therefore, is our reflective self as concerned with matters of moral choice: things that make us uneasy (scruples, guilts) or things that beckon as prospective goods (further growth, more beauty, or love). It is a precious faculty or dimension of the self, a direct line of access to the Spirit of God. Indeed, when we grow mature in conscience we become religiously adult, people of use to Christ and the cause of the gospel.

## Christian Faith in the Spirit

The reflective awareness that makes us distinctly human orients us toward Mystery. The world we survey, when we reflect on our sensible experience and our store of insights into its meaning, is limitless. There is the outreach of the astronomical world, spanning galaxy after galaxy. There is the bottomless world of the nuclear particles, like boxes within boxes within boxes. The human body poses biologists and physicians ten questions for every answer their brilliant research brings forth. The human psyche keeps counselors, artists, poets, and theologians stocked with more stimuli than they can factor. Nature, society, and the self all point "beyond," saying that their complexity will never yield a simple explanation of how they came to be. The basic question in philosophy therefore remains what it has been for centuries: Why is there something rather than nothing? What gives the world its being and form?

The Christian instinct is to answer these questions with a shy smile. From faith in Jesus, Christians have an inventory of concepts that address such questions, but they know instinctively that no concepts, however accurate, will ever do the real job. The answers to the ultimate questions about the world's being and form all compress into "God." But God is not just another being, another bead in the endless string. God is the fullness of being, the source that needs no other. So the concepts generated by Christian minds over the centuries quickly cede to the holistic faith welling up in Christian hearts. Making their own Jesus' attitude toward the God he called "Abba," the Christian saints have treated the foundation of the world, the "answer" to the comprehensive question implied in a nature, society, and self that do not explain themselves, as an infinite yet intimate Love. The real God who is equal to the task of explaining the galaxies and mesons is bound to overspill our minds. Our minds are but little measuring cups; the Ultimate Reality is a limitless ocean.

Our hearts, though, can reach beyond our minds, should God choose to move them. In the ultimate zone of things, the usual law that love follows on knowledge can suffer a striking reverse:

> It used to be said, *Nihil amatum nisi praecognitum,* Knowledge precedes love. . . . But the major exception to the Latin tag is God's gift of his love flooding our hearts. Then we are in the dynamic state of being in love. But who it is we love, is neither given nor yet understood. Our capacity for moral self-transcendence [ethical growth] has found a fulfillment that brings deep joy and profound peace. Our love reveals to us values we had not appreciated, values of prayer and worship, or repentance and belief. But if we would learn what is going on within us, if we would learn to integrate it with the rest of our living, we have to inquire, investigate, seek counsel. So it is that in religious matters love precedes knowledge and, as that love is God's gift, the very beginning of faith is due to God's gift.[1]

When the Ultimate Reality gives us a love of life, a reverent appreciation for the universe in which we've been placed, we are moved to contend with the answer to our deepest questions as an affair of the heart. Christians believe that God offers all human beings this love of life and life's foundations, is for all human beings present as the mysterious affair of the heart into which all their questions and aspirations flow. By virtue of Christ's teaching and resurrection, they believe that the Holy Spirit, God's promised "Helper," buoys the hearts of all people, would lead the consciences of all people toward light and life. So, in Christian perspective, the scruples we experience, as our longings to be better, are touches of the Holy Spirit. Those who resist these touches withdraw toward a sterile or self-twisting isolation. Those who try to respond, opening their hearts to the world's beauty or following their sense of responsibility or answering the call to alleviate pain, gradually have seep into their being an incalculable peace and joy. Although they never understand the Mystery of the whole, in virtue of this peace and joy they begin to believe that it is a Love to which they can surrender, a Goodness to which they can say, "Yes!"

One can read of such yea-saying in the lives of many people, humble as well as eminent. If the diaries of the eminent Danish diplomat Dag Hammarskjöld record a moment when he broke through his near-despair to say a simple yes of self-surrender, the diaries of Pearl Tull, the nearly no-account, highly flawed woman created by novelist Anne Tyler, record a perfect moment when what Christians call "the Spirit" taught her the goodness of her life:

> *"February sixth, nineteen-ten,"* Ezra [Pearl's son] read aloud. *"I baked a few Scottish Fancies but they wouldn't do to take to a tea."*
>
> His mother, listening intently, thought that over a while. Then she made her gesture of dismissal and started rocking again in her rocker.
>
> *"I hitched up Prince and rode downtown for brown silk gloves and an ice bag. Then got out my hat frames and washed my straw hat. For supper fixed a batch of—"*
>
> "Move on," his mother said.
>
> He riffled through the pages, glimpsing *buttonhole stitch* and *watermelon social* and *set of fine furs for $22.50.* *"Early this morning,"* he read to his mother, *"I went out behind the house to weed. Was kneeling in the dirt by the stable with my pinafore a mess and the perspiration rolling down my back, wiped my face on my sleeve, reached for the trowel, and all at once thought, Why I believe that at just this moment I am absolutely happy."*
>
> His mother stopped rocking and grew very still.
>
> *"The Bedloe girl's piano scales were floating out her window,"* he read, *"and a bottle fly was buzzing in the grass, and I saw that I was kneeling on such a beautiful green little planet. I don't care what else might come about, I have had this moment. It belongs to me."*
>
> That was the end of the entry. He fell silent.
>
> "Thank you, Ezra," his mother said. "There's no need to read any more."[2]

## *The Complexity of Contemporary Life*

Pearl Tull's perfect moment stands out from the surrounding trivia of her diaries like a diamond from a pile of mulch. It is the one recollection able to comfort her as she faces the meager accomplishments of her many years and the close drawing-near of her death.

We contemporary Americans have to struggle to estimate the peculiarity of our culture, but probably it is not completely romantic nostalgia for us to suspect that premodern peoples had many more moments of diamondlike brilliance. For example, even into the twentieth century a researcher such as the depth psychologist C. G. Jung could find traditional peoples like the Pueblo Indians of the American Southwest who were mesmerized by natural phenomena that gave their lives brilliant meaning:

> As I sat with Ochwiay Biano on the roof, the blazing sun rising higher and higher, he said, pointing to the sun, "Is not he who moves there our father? How can anyone say differently? How can there be another god? Nothing can be without the sun." His excitement, which was already perceptible, mounted still higher; he struggled for words, and exclaimed at last, "What would a man do alone in the mountains? He cannot even build his fire without him."[3]

For the Pueblo Indian Ochwiay Biano, the daily rising of the sun was an inexhaustible wonder. Living high in the mountains, his people believed that their prayers helped the sun to climb above the horizon and so contributed to the maintenance of the world. Were they to falter in their religious rites, the system of the world might well break down. Their lives therefore had an unimpeachable significance: They collaborated with the ultimate powers of the universe to keep the system of the world going. No doubt particular experiences held special revelations and certain moments in the life cycle were key. But the whole Pueblo pattern of working and recreating, praying and playing, was fitted to a clear, objective, and divine order. These people did not have to scratch their heads and tug their beards to find their lives' direction. The world in which they were physically set, as partners obviously small and subordinate, gave them more splendor and meaning than their wisest tribal member would be able to fathom in the longest lifetime.

Merely to sketch such a traditional, premodern world

view is to suggest how radically our contemporary American culture departs from the convictions of 99 percent of the historical generations that preceded us. Only with the rise of modern science did the traditional view that physical nature obviously frames our human lives fall away from the center of a sizeable portion of human beings' cultures. But fallen away it has, so most of us in the technological nations now live without a secure sense of our lives' meaning. Neither the rising of the sun nor the rising of the moon intimates religious mysteries. Neither time nor tide is a medium in which we can float assured of our lives' significance. Cut off from the states of soul that took traditional human beings to the central Mystery of creation, most of our contemporaries search willy-nilly through the waste-baskets of their lives, grateful to come up with one golden moment. If they find one, and they have any wisdom at all, they clutch it to their bosoms as a treasure. But a great many, completely brainwashed by contemporary trends, would shake their heads and tell themselves the very notion of a treasure is illusory, the golden moment has to be fool's gold. In the dominant streams of contemporary American culture, both high and low, there are no privileged moments, no exits into sacred Mystery. The world is not sacramental. One is extraordinary to have recognized a moment of absolute happiness.

How utterly this contemporary nihilism contrasts with the Christian world view and the Christian convictions about the Spirit! For while the Christian world view and convictions are far from identical to those of traditional peoples like the Pueblos, Christians share with traditional peoples a faith that the world does give forth a numinous shine, the world's seasons and creations are vestiges and icons of a Holy Power. Smohalla, the nineteenth-century American Indian who would not plow the earth, because that would have been like driving a knife into the bosom of his mother, would have understood the refrain of Genesis 1 that after God's acts of creation "God saw that it was good."

Smohalla wouldn't have suspected that this was an important refrain in the white man's heritage, so ravaging had the whites shown themselves. But he could have walked many miles with whites who knew their Genesis. The biblical writ given human beings to subdue the earth (Gen. 1:28) is hardly a warrant for the earth's ravishment. Our crying need for a new theology of nature today is but one expression of the confusion that came when we lost our sense of the Creator Spirit.[4]

Contemporary life is unbearably complex because seldom do its reams of data find a counterweight in a deep contemplative simplicity. We are confused because we live almost exclusively on the surface of our minds, midst the flotsam and jetsam of the news, and virtually never visit our clear depths. The politics, family life, church busyness, and pop culture into which we have plunged bear us no satisfying design, no simple cut to the heart of the matter. The God who might bring the whole to order, give the turning world a still point, is so pale a stranger we're hardly aware how much we suffer for not knowing him. Where many prior peoples hungered to know God more than they hungered for bread, we fill vast storehouses with loaves of air. What fools: This night our souls may be required of us, and then whose will our delicacies be?

## The Hunger for Wholeness

That is a rather harsh reading of contemporary American life, written in a mood of disgust with its so many trivializations. To be fair I should add the more positive signs, the evidences that many people do feel surfeited with nonessentials, hungry for a stripped, bare, God-centered life. The novelist Mary Gordon speaks for some of these people when she has one of her characters say:

> I am interested in the perception of the sacred. So many humans seem to hunger for it: the clear, the unencumbered. I too hunger, but my hunger is specific. If I could see the face of God as free from all necessity, the vision as the reward of a

grueling search, the soul stripped down, rock hard, then I would look for him. The pure light that enlightens [everyone]. If [God] would show himself so, then I would seek him. But I will not let him into my heart. My daughter is there, my mother, Leo, Cyprian, the women whom I love. I will not open my heart to God. If he is the only God I could worship, he will value my chastity. But I will not be violated; I will not submit myself. I will wait. But I will wait for light, not love.[5]

This character is representative of many sensitive people in wanting to attain something clear and unencumbered. She is representative of only a few (usually quite young and highly educated) people in putting such rigorous conditions on what God or the sacred must be. For the majority of us, God must be love and life even more than light. Perhaps because we have some acquaintance with the confluence of love, life, and light in the Johannine writings of the New Testament, we sense that the foundation of the world, the source of wholeness for the world and ourselves, must be all three. In terms of the traditional Christian theology of the Trinity, this conjures the Father (life), the Son (light), and the Spirit (love). The God who would make us and the world orderly and fulfilled is a community in which our peak symbols (generated by our peak experiences) have a substantial and unlimited reality. Were this to be the God we could hope to meet in our depths, we might have powerful reasons for leaving our superficiality and trying to pray deeply.

And, of course, this is the God. The ultimate that offers Itself in grace is the Trinitarian community of Father-Son-Spirit, the unlimited substantial reality of Life-Light-Love. Eastern Christianity has done a better job of mining the riches of scripture and the riches of the early church fathers that carry this theme than Western Christianity. In the theologies of both Greek and Russian Orthodox Christianity, *grace* primarily means the divine, Trinitarian life. Those who are baptized into Christ become partakers of the divine nature:

His divine power has granted to us all things that pertain to life and godliness, through the knowledge of him who called

> us to his own glory and excellence, by which he has granted
> to us his precious and very great promises, that through these
> you may escape from the corruption that is in the world be-
> cause of passion and become partakers of the divine nature.
> —2 Peter 1:3–4

So the hunger that many of us exhibit, our thirst for living water unadulterated by passion or selfishness, is in faith's view a desire to partake in God's own life. The God who has left witness everywhere is trying to show us the greater fullness of life we could find if we would leave our worldly passions and open ourselves to the divine Mysteries.

From this perspective (of the theology of grace), the struggles of conscience that we go through are more than just exercises in character building or good citizenship. What is at issue in our choices for honesty or cheating, selfishness or generosity, fidelity or adultery is opening or closing to the Mystery of God, the offer of divine life. It certainly helps to have this offer clarified by the revelation of Jesus and to place oneself in the midst of the Christian church. But there are people outside the church who are responding generously to God's grace and people inside the church who have closed themselves. Indeed, the sinfulness and closure of many churchgoers is a prime stumbling block to those weighing the claims of the gospel, just as the goodness and openness of many churchgoers is a prime attraction. Wholeness requires a willingness to keep going, keep putting off selfishness and sloth. Many more people wish they were whole than are willing to work hard to become whole. Inside and outside the church, the number of fully realized personalities is small. (The psychologist Abraham Maslow found that only about 1 percent of the people he studied could be described as fully realized: living at anything near their peak capacity.)

Still, the Spirit keeps alive our images of perfection, our hopes for a better self, family, and world. Until we become completely despairing (and few of us do), the chance to get away and relax revives our convictions that it's not completely hopeless. The kids (or the weather or a success at work) come through with an unexpected bit of sunshine and our toil again seems worthwhile. I remember the joy of the parents of three teenagers as they told of coming home to find their kids calmly handling a crisis caused by a thunderstorm. Whereas previously the kids had been irresponsible to the point of driving the parents to tears of frustration, in this pinch the teenagers had started the sump pump, cleaned up the cellar, and saved hundreds of dollars worth of furniture and clothing from ruin. Whatever inspiration or grace caused them to come through was much more important to their parents than to themselves. The parents had been desperate for a sign that they would ever succeed in raising creatures recognizably human, and the kids gave them a technicolor billboard.

## Immersion and Withdrawal

As the reference to getting away and relaxing (as an occasion for having one's hopes revive) suggests, the spiritual life has fairly regular rhythms. One of the most significant wisdoms of biblical religion is the notion of a sabbath, a day of rest and religious observance. Simply by putting a limit to toil and this-worldly business, many Jews and Christians have kept the world a creature, defeated the so many tendencies within them and outside them that would have made the world an idol. Although we must earn our bread by the sweat of our brow, this hard work must not become our only interest. The first commandment, after all, is to love the Lord, our God, with whole mind, heart, soul, and strength. It is true that work directed toward God, offered to God, can be a form of such love, a matter of obedience to the first commandment. However, both Jewish and Christian masters of the spiritual life have not found work alone to be enough. Unless we also pray, play, study, and celebrate we will not be full creatures and our love of God will not be wholehearted. Thus every day, week, and year of the traditional Jewish and

Christian calendars made provision for expressing love of God in ways other than work.

What this suggests to me, in this context of an examination of Christian conscience, is the significance of a rhythm of immersion and withdrawal. For most of us, immersion is a necessity, as well as something relatively congenial. We must work, do business, take care of kids, shoulder part of the load in our neighborhood and at church—and we *want* to do our share, feel good when we are asked to be responsible and can answer generously. The middle years of the life cycle are driven by a need to be needed, an energy to make our mark, prop our community. A few solitary people are exceptions to this rule, but they are only a small fraction of the population. For most of us, immersion is natural, acceptable, something to which we've long been accustomed.

Still, it would profit us to take a look at how other cultures have conceived of their peoples' maturation. The two dominant cultures of the East, the Indian and the Chinese, have balanced immersion in family life, business, and community affairs with regular withdrawal. In the traditional Indian (Hindu) conception of the life cycle, the young person first was apprenticed to a guru to learn the scriptures (Vedas) and self-discipline. Then he (the pattern often did not hold for women) would return to his family, marry, and assume secular responsibilities. But when the hair of his head had turned gray and he saw his children's children, he would withdraw from secular affairs, begin taking stock of his life and meditating more profoundly. If this meditation and withdrawal produced its ideal fruit, he would become an enlightened sage and wander with virtually no possessions, teaching others the supreme value of religious insight.

The customary Chinese life cycle was not staged so formally, but it also made definite provision for withdrawal and meditation. The slogan for educated Chinese was, "In office a Confucian, in retirement a Taoist." This meant that in daily affairs, business, social relations, and the like, one ought to hew to the rather formal, highly ritualized and hierarchical views of the Confucians (who dominated both governmental and family thinking). However, in the recreational side of one's life, the places where one tried to nurture a private or artistic self, the more poetic and mystical Taoists were the best guides. Retirement in our sense of ceasing formal participation in the work world meant for most Chinese a fuller preoccupation with the Taoist ideal of harmonizing oneself with the Way that ran through nature and society. The Confucian custom of withdrawing for three years of mourning at the death of a parent dovetailed with the Taoist sentiments, giving all Chinese a right to take time to think, ponder what they had become by middle age, prepare for the responsibilities they would face in the second half of life (when they were supposed to be models for the younger generation).

We in the West have not developed such clear guidelines for how to mature through the life cycle. This lack in our tradition has come home to roost in modern times, giving us little defense against workaholism. A majority of our people spend their first sixty years immersed in doing, hardly at all concerned with being. So even our weekends tend to be rushed, as filled with recreational doings as our weekdays are filled with the doings of work. Some of us instinctively take fallow time, intuiting that without this our creativity would thin disastrously, but few of us, in the population as a whole, have developed a happy regime that sets "office" and "retirement" into a stimulating counterpoint, gives our days, weeks, and years a rhythm as steady and fruitful as nature's own. Few of us capitalize on the natural quiet of early morning and late evening to tally our accounts, examine our consciences, beg God's aid for the battles to come or thank God for help in the battles concluded. Western monks did this through their canonical hours of prayer, but the majority of modern Christians have not received a monastic training.

One of my themes in this book, then, will be the great value of making one's life rhythmic. For a Christian conscience to mature, it must become reflective and contemplative. It will best do this, I believe, if it establishes a rhythm of immersion in doing and withdrawal to concentrate on being, plunging into experience and stepping back to take stock of what one is becoming, how one is performing.

2.

# THE LURE OF REFLECTION

## *In the Beginning Is Wonder*

If it is correct to think that, for a rhythmic arrangement of our time, most of us would have to factor in more withdrawal, the best way to make such withdrawal attractive might be to stress its wonder-ful side. Reflection is something natural, right, proper to human beings, something that so exercises a basic part of our makeup that it feels good. The lure of reflection can get snagged on distractions and extroversions, however, and never dangle before our inner spirits, let alone hook us into the process of exploring our souls. In most cases where people do become significantly reflective, it is powerful experiences of wonder that have cleared out such distractions and extroversions. Being struck by something beautiful, or troubled by something threatening, or mesmerized by something intellectually challenging, we are almost forced to begin the spiritual life, the quest for meaning and wholeness. For this reason, Aristotle said that the beginning of the life that is in love with wisdom (the life that he called *philosophy*) is wonder *(thaumazein).*

Aristotle also said that all people by nature desire to know. If we correlate these two Aristotelian sayings, we

26

have the solid foundation of a theory of learning applicable to all sorts of education, initiation into the Christian spiritual life quite included. I remember standing in the middle of the street outside my house (it was not a very busy street) struck by a completely new thought. I was perhaps nine years old and various things had been troubling me. There were problems at home (alcoholism and a scarcity of money) and problems at school (bullies threatening to beat me up). I wanted to cry, or talk to someone, or run away—anything that would lessen the panic and confusion. Suddenly I realized that I was not completely defenseless. Under the pressure of my great need to get some answers, some handle on my situation, my mind pivoted and faced me with the fact that I could *think* about my situation, master it by understanding.

This was such a new concept that my mouth fell open and I stopped in midstride. Suddenly I was no longer a slave of all my fears, an animal running through thickets or mazes of other peoples' devising. I did not use these notions or illustrations, of course. I had only my little nine-year-old's equivalents (I can plan for Dad's not coming home, I can make sure I'm never alone with the bullies). But I distinctly remember being more fascinated by the core of my discovery than by any of its practical applications. A whole new dimension of myself had opened up. My interiority had dropped its veil and stood beckoning as a wonderland ripe for exploring. My spirits soared and I probably tugged up my socks. As I look back, it seems to me that that experience, that shock of wonder and lure of discovery, was my rite of passage from childhood to adulthood. To be sure, I still had all the psychosexual changeover of adolescence to traverse. But, however precociously, after that experience I was in an essential way an adult. A tough yet lightsome little crystal-core of me had precipitated out of my turmoils and driven away the bogies. Ever since, I've had a surprise for the condescending types who have presumed to try to take over my life. "Don't tread on me," a small still voice has barked. "I'm quite capable of handling my own affairs."

The wonder that made me reflective was occasioned by the particular trials of my boyhood. Other people report different seductions into the spiritual life. Patrick White's wonderful novel *The Vivesector,* for instance, shows a little boy fascinated by light.[1] The glitter of a chandelier completely absorbs him, shunting him onto an artistic pathway that determines the rest of his life. Because he is a person of depth, willing to confront his considerable sufferings, this pathway becomes religious, even mystical. (He might not use these terms, but White leaves no doubt about the parallels to the classical *via negativa* or way of darkness and unknowing.) Anne Tyler's similar artistic character, Jeremy Pauling, is fascinated by color. To work out his collages and sculptures he will go without food, neglect his family, live the life of an eccentric barely able to cope with ordinary matters of survival.[2]

These fictional characters are more remarkable than the people we meet around the neighborhood, but only because art always dramatizes the ordinary into something special. People who absorb themselves with science or cooking or teaching or medicine or even football or auto repair find in such passionate interests something wonderful, fascinating, ecstatic, and fulfilling. A skillful spiritual director could take such wonder and make it the entryway to a spiritual path of self-knowledge. "What is it about professional football that so intrigues you?" she might ask. "What do you think your pleasure in watching a perfect play unfold says about the build of your personality?" If the football fan responded, the spiritual director could beckon him or her into the labyrinth of the spirit and start guiding that person through the twists and turns we must pass if we are to come to the center of ourselves.

## Coming to Understand

Wonder has value in its own right, is good simply for occurring, but it does not exist in isolation. The antecedents of wonder include the sensations and memories that fall into a constellation that gives us pause, and the consequences can be significant insights. When a sensation or an image or a memory has caught our attention, drawn our interest, made us wonder, we begin to itch to understand. The scientist who labors for years tucked away in a laboratory usually is driven by a desire to understand. The man in the street turning over the tumult of his domestic life keeps trying to get a handle on the problem. When understanding does occur, the release of tension it brings tells us how much we had invested in searching. If we have been working on a significant problem, something either objectively important or of great moment in our personal life, getting the point, catching on, having things fall into place is enormously fulfilling. The clouds vanish and light floods the land. Our senses quicken and adrenaline fills us with energy. Not only do all people by nature desire to know, knowing tells all people a large part of what they have been made for.

Impressed by the power of understanding, the medieval theologians worked out a view of heaven in which understanding would be the central activity. In a "beatific vision" of God, the person would enjoy an endless, ongoing penetration of the infinite divine being. This would mean a constant experience of the sort of light that had flashed in the person's most powerful acts of understanding. There would be no question of becoming bored, because the divine nature is limitless and understanding is intrinsically fulfilling. To grasp something of the cause or explanation of the universe would be the most radical sort of understanding and fulfillment. It would never exhaust the Mystery of God. The divine incomprehensibility would make the eternity of heaven constantly wonderful. The intellectual need of human beings to pass from wonder to understanding is so great that without full understanding there would be no "heaven." (Equally, heaven would fulfill our need for limitless love, but some of the medievals—most prominently the Thomists—preferred to stress understanding.)[3]

The clearest acts of understanding probably are

mathematical. Take the following series of numbers: 5, 25, 50, 48, 24, 26, 676, 1352, 1350, 675, ____. Assume that the series has a pattern. What number ought to go into the blank spot? If you have understood the pattern, you know that the missing number is 677. You also know the pattern: squared, times two, minus two, divided by two, plus two, repeated beginning with squared. The moment when you grasped the pattern brought you a small flash of light. If you did not grasp the pattern, did not understand the logic of the series, you got no flash of light. If you tried to crack the problem, spent any time and energy at all on it, you marshalled your wits, narrowed your attention, started to suffer a certain irritation or impatience or frustration. If you labored in frustration for some time and then had the light flash, you probably felt almost inordinately pleased with yourself. Although you knew that this was a trivial problem, composed only as an illustration, it had gotten on your nerves, become a personal challenge. Therefore when you forced it to yield an answer you won a little victory.

Each day millions of people work crossword puzzles, acrostics, and the like in search of little victories. Millions more work a less tractable problem, searching for a way to live—organize their time, spend their money, relate to their spouse, boss, friends, kids—that would be lightsome, clean, efficient, satisfying. The problem of *life* so seldom admits of a clear solution that many people come to the peculiar insight that life doesn't have the sort of intelligibility that a crossword puzzle or an engineering problem or balancing one's checkbook does. Life is too comprehensive, detailed, irregular for us to grasp its pattern in one brilliant insight. Indeed, the problem of life is so closely related to the problem of God (the causal basis of life) that to solve it would be to be in heaven, possessed of the beatific vision. But to be hungry to understand life, and know that only in heaven could one understand life, is to realize that human time before heaven is intrinsically frustrating. One must find ways other than the narrowly intellectual to cope with life's intractability. Perhaps the ways traditionally called *faith* or *prayer* or *mysticism* can supply.

The people who get this far into the implications of understanding, or just of wanting to understand, probably are relatively few. Such a journey requires the inclination to reflect about wonder and insight and the education to link this reflection with the global issues of life's meaning and God. But the reflection that even rudimentary efforts to follow up on wondering or understanding bring into play is a powerhouse for the Christian conscience. When it is tutored to examine its orientation to the light, its limitations, and its other resources for comprehensive coping (such as feelings and invitations to faith), our reflective faculty becomes impressively moral, asking us to act as though we were beings with a limited but real capacity for understanding. Indeed, it implies that not to try to understand, not to put our minds to work, is to shirk an obligation at the core of our humanity. Such a shirking would make us inauthentic, underdeveloped, pots that give the potter pain. It would amount to burying our talents in a field and denying that our Master expects a rich yield.

## Testing Our Insights

When our puzzling over a problem brings a flash of understanding, the concept that expresses this understanding is hypothetical. For example, if you labored over the number series laid out in the last section and came up with the formula that explained it, you had an ordering that you could think *might* prove to do the job. Until you took that formula (squared, times two, minus two, divided by two, plus two, repeat) and checked it, verifying that it actually did do the job, your understanding was incomplete. You could be enthusiastic that you probably had cracked the problem, but you could not be sure or wholly confident.

The difference between *might* and *is,* as any person of experience knows, is enormous. There might have been green cheese on the moon, but scientific analysis and the tramp of the astronauts showed that there neither was nor could be. I may be going to make a billion dollars by getting my fleet of pedal-powered planes into the air and onto Wall Street, but then again I may not. I thought that the boss might be preparing me for higher things by his needling and sarcasm, until I found the pink slip in my box.

The gap between insights yielding hypotheses and verifications yielding solid understandings that we can act upon is no less crucial in the spiritual life or the domain of conscience. Before we can be secure in thinking that Christian church membership is helpful or even obligatory, we have to try it for a while, see what its actual living produces. Before we can be sure that the path of prayer is sweetness and light, we have to hang in there for a couple of years, learn whether the transitions and testings that the traditional masters describe won't come to apply in our case. This sort of prudence and reserve is not the negativity of the skeptic, the fear of the person too timid to take a flyer, the lack of imagination of the person covered with mud from being stuck. It is the good sense of the person who at least intuits (if she does not know expressly) how her mind works, what is necessary before she can say in good conscience that something is so, has proven solid, can be touted to others as reliable.

This good sense separates the wise elder from the young car salesman. Of our wise elders we require judiciousness, an instinct to ponder and sift. In our caricatures of car salesmen as types to beware, we sketch in flashy clothes, a glib tongue, quick moves that feel little obligation to walk the straight and narrow. From the legions of such salespeople filing down its columns, history has minted the sterling advice, *Caveat emptor*! Let the buyer beware, because the seller is concerned, too many times, not with what is so but with what will get by as the appearance of what is so, the glitter of a good deal rather than the substance of a good product.

Once again, analogies in the business of religion are

both easy to find and quite relevant. Let the prospective buyers of Christian religion who shop the airwaves beware of the glitter of crystal cathedrals, the glibness of Bible spouters, the deft hands of easy healers. Let them do a little Bible versing of their own, recalling that it is easier for a camel to pass through the eye of a needle than for a rich person to enter the kingdom of God, that the way of the Christ did not circumvent suffering, that Christ's healings both required faith and intended the glory of God. The long Christian tradition of testing things in the Spirit argues that we seldom need rush into precipitous decision, almost always have time to let God's will become clear. Sufficient for each day is the evil thereof.

Christian conscience matures by the weighing, sifting, waiting on the Spirit, watching and praying that we sketch when we compose our idealizations of the spiritual masters. In the Christian case, as well as the classical Greek case that the tragedian Aeschylus summarized, wisdom comes through suffering. People who have not undergone, felt personally, had to cope, walked in the dark, been brought to God out of naked need are not fully credentialed. They may have much talent, be good raw material, but until they have emerged from such testing they are still in training. When Aristotle gave the opinion that one needs fifty years of living to become good at ethical theory, he built on his realization that prudential wisdom only develops through experience. Bright as a person may be, he or she will not know what is fitting in particular cases until so many cases have passed by, been worked through, that almost any new one will be analogous to ones already seen. On the way to reaching the mature human being whose practice is the concrete ethical norm, much living and much reflecting were Aristotle's prescription.

Similarly, on the way to the saint, much living, praying, and reflecting have been the traditional prescription. The first notions one forms of the Christian life have to be assayed in the furnace of daily endurance, so that the gold can separate from the dross. The purgative way has to yield to the illuminative way, where the biblical truths come alive, take on the sharp cut of personal relevance, start to serve as equipment that can make our conversion useful. And then the illuminative way in turn has to yield to the unitive way, through a process of stripping in which all concepts are relativized, shown to be inadequate, bracketed lest they interfere with the Spirit's direct leading. Insight is an important beginning, but testing is where realism builds its muscle.

## Going Deep in Judgment

The part of the reflective survey that moves us from hypotheses to realities that is most crucial for Christian conscience is the self-examination that occurs prior to our best judgments. In matters of moral import, when we have to decide among competing values, the prospective course of action that looms as that which *might* be best only becomes that which we are confident *is* best after we have reviewed not only the insights that led to its proposal but also our own biases and self-interests. This review can tell us two important things about our own build or makeup.

First, it can tell us that we are knowers, do have the competence to handle experience and work it through to something trustworthy. When we weigh the evidence, verify our processes of insight, reach down toward the sufficiency of reason that will produce the understanding and conviction that we have attained what is so, what is true, we find that attaining what is so, reaching what is true, is at the inmost core of our humanity. We are proportioned to the things presented in our experience, and they are proportioned to us. There is a similarity between us as knowers and them as knowables. In Christian terms, this is a concrete experience of the light that enlightens everyone born into the world (John 1:9).

Second, the review that precedes responsible judgments can tell us that dispassion is our best judgmental mood and so is a prime characteristic of our selves when they are at their most realistic. Unless we are dispassionate, free of inordinate emotions, we cannot weigh the evidence accurately, get to the clear bottom of our limpid ability to know. Passions roil the waters, stir up much on the bottom. They are necessary for fighting evils and pursuing goods enthusiastically but, as the proverbs of most peoples make plain, they are bad counselors when it comes to important judgments. So it is a fool who is his own lawyer, a fool who rushes in where angels fear to tread, a fool who marries in haste and must repent at leisure. If you get a letter that turns you livid, you should put it in your bottom drawer, be sure not to answer it until next week. If you are flying high with religious consolation, you should remember that last week you were low and hangdog, lest you think yourself superhuman and make commitments you cannot honor.

The proverbial literature of the Bible is a good specimen of the sober, at times almost dour and cynical, mood that deep reflectiveness can induce. In the Bible one usually finds a reservoir of hope, since the ultimate disposition of things lies in God's hands, but the writers of the Wisdom Literature are not optimists. They know that the wellsprings of good judgment are hard to reach, because it has taken them much labor to get there. They know that without the guidance of the Spirit of God, human beings are almost bound to miss the mark. To come to the calm wisdom of a Solomon, and be inspired to realize that the true or worthy mother of the child would always prefer the child's good to her own, is a rare happening indeed. Wisdom is a gift of God. The best preparation we can make to receive it is inner cleansing, expectant listening, holding ourselves ready to catch where the wind presently is willing to blow.

*Dispassion*, then, is another word for purity of heart, which, as Kierkegaard made plain, means to will only one thing: what is true and godly. Until we have been able to put aside what we want to be true, what we insist should be godly, our hearts are impure. We are the pots, not the potter. Mature Christian consciences love the will of God, not the fancies of the self. Quietly waiting, patiently trying to keep its medium clear, the religious conscience asks the Mystery that holds all the truly important answers to vouchsafe a word. We are listeners for a word, petitioners for the Word. The Incarnation comes as the almost excessive granting by God of a demand built into our beings. As spiritual creatures, we can survey the heavens, map a universe, and dimly conceive the Mystery of the whole. As material creatures we do all this symbolically, with debts to our bodies that we can never outrun. So the answer that suits our condition is a form of Mystery's self-disclosure that we can see, hear, touch, taste, smell, imagine, remember. The word for which we wait in all our important judgmental processes, the symbol that can summarize the course of action that seems best, is a miniature of God's Word, the infinite and eternal self-expression that condescended to take flesh and become available in space and time.

When Augustine said that God is more intimate to us than we are to ourselves, he was implying all this richness. At the still point of our inner world, when dispassion has stopped the turning, we find the immensity of God to be an ocean on which our spirits rest. We also find the Incarnation of God to be a fine point or small still voice that gives the ocean order and contour. Going deep in judgment finally is indistinguishable from prayer. The depths of consciousness are the depths of conscience, because our awareness finally is that we are creatures formed by God and invited, required, to respond. So the vectors of responsibility, the calls to become sober (not grim) and judicious, are calls of God in our consciousness and conscience. When we are led to our depths, the Spirit has us in hand for a Christian education.

## Feeling Right with God

The openness that comes when we take the Spirit's hand, try at least to become pure of heart and will only one thing, makes possible the substantial fulfillment of our personalities. We are made with a quasi-infinity of intellectual and emotional capacity. No amount of knowledge exhausts our capacity to know. No amount of love exhausts our capacity to love. The limits (of time, energy, strength) that we suffer all flow from our material nature. In the spiritual center of ourselves, we are candidates for a beatific vision, a quieting of our restless hearts by Infinite Goodness itself. To be open to the real (if mysterious) God at the depths of conscience is to anticipate the fulfillment of heaven. When the Spirit moves to fill our openness, give our hearts loving rest, we have the guarantee or downpayment of which Second Corinthians (1:22; 5:5) speaks. This makes us feel right with God, hope that we are justified.

Our feeling right with God is not, of course, something we can boast about. It is God's doing, not our own. There is no certainty of our salvation, only the certainty that God will never stop loving us. Nothing can separate us from the love of God—not because we cannot become unlovable, but because God cannot become unloving. So the feelings of rightness that we have when the Spirit lists (inclines) are reliable because we may, on the testimony of scripture and Christian tradition, interpret them as signs of grace. They are not prods to self-righteousness but prods to humility and gratitude. We always remain unprofitable servants. Even when we water and plant, only God gives the increase. This is not because God has to be top dog, doesn't want to share the glory. The Greek Father Irenaeus believed God so wants to share the glory that God's glory is the sight of human beings fully alive. No, only God can give the increase because the increase is strictly a matter of grace: the divine life of Father-Son-Spirit that exceeds all human natures.

By turns, then, we arrive at the point where the humility and gratitude we feel, as the inevitable overflow of a right relation with God at our centers, are the dispositions of a family member. Freely, without any claim on our part, God has taken us up into the inner

Trinitarian life. The sharing in the divine nature that Second Peter 1:4 mentions has been conceived by Eastern Christian theology as a process of divinization *(theosis)*. God's love is so far-reaching that it wants to transform us, to make us capable of receiving the divine Self (Trinitarian reality).

What we human lovers yearn after, God has in perfect form by nature: complete compenetration. This compenetration, which the Christian theological tradition has called *perichoresis* or *circumincessio,* means that Father, Son, and Spirit are both perfectly distinct and perfectly united. They differ relationally (Father is the unbegotten source, Son is the begotten image, Spirit is the breathed-forth love), but they share completely the one divine nature. So they are three "persons" (not finite identities, as human persons are) but not three gods. It is this perfect community or society of life, light, and love that grace makes available to us. God offers us the divine Self. Our consciousnesses open onto the Mystery—the divine creative love as revealed, inviting us into its "inside." No longer is the relation simply Creator to creature (if that would imply lack of access to God's innermost, Trinitarian "personality"). It is now Lover to beloved, Parent to child, Friend to friend: "No longer do I call you servants, for the servant does not know what his master is doing; but I have called you friends, for all that I have heard from my Father I have made known to you" (John 15:15).

Now, I have taken this excursion into Trinitarian theology not, I hope, simply to dangle theological esoterica but to suggest at least a fraction of the riches that Christian tradition has found at the depths of conscience. We are more God's than our own, and that by several titles. We are creatures, who exist only by God's fiat. We are sinners, who stand right with God only by Christ's arduous redemptive labors. And we are children of God, sharers in the divine nature, by the love of God poured forth in our hearts by the Holy Spirit, the decision of the Godhead to come and make its dwelling with us. It is the worst impoverishment to neglect these riches of the theology of grace and consider Christian religious education, Christian ethics, or Christian formation of conscience as though they were only a matter of mastering certain rules, memorizing one's obligations to the church, or becoming legalistic about the implications of the Ten Commandments. Christian conscience is far simpler, richer, and more demanding than that. We are called to be as good as God, because we are called, invited, almost seduced to open up and share God's life.

So the rightness we experience when we visit our depths and open everything to God is God's doing. Like everything else of significance, it is God's in its initiation, ground, and consummation. We can say yes or no to the process. God does not coerce our agreement, force our love. But God does show us the stance that Yahweh showed Israel. As Hosea, for example, found, God let himself be heartsick over Israel, made himself vulnerable to the point of feeling the way a husband would if the wife he loved utterly was unfaithful. The rightness we feel when we try to open ourselves from the center is the embrace of a lover absolutely tactful, powerful, and faithful. God can no more abandon us than Hosea could abandon Gomer, Yahweh could abandon Israel, a nursing mother could abandon her child.

# 3.

# THE PRACTICE OF REFLECTION

## *Orientation in the Morning*

We have spent no little time on the lure of reflection: reasons why and ways in which it might be attractive, a good thing, to turn back, center down, and ponder our experience. In this chapter we focus on ways of being reflective: how to do it, what it might feel like, what likely would occur. The basic framework for this more practical and descriptive discussion will be the poles of the day, morning and night. Most of us rise in the morning and retire at night. If reflection could capitalize on the format of morning to evening, it would be off to a fine start.

Now that we have passed the autumnal equinox, I rise in the dark. I like to rise in the dark (except in winter, when it is very cold), because the dark seems to enhance the quiet. Also, if I wish I can wait and watch for the dawn, taking in my breath as first the purple and then the rose spreads across the eastern horizon. For years, when I was in the seminary, a bothersome bell summoned us to rise at 5:30. I don't know whether this habituation discovered my love of early morning or created it, but the fact now is that the first hour of the day is the one I love best. (Sometimes I have to fight the

40

feeling that after breakfast it's all down hill.) The first hour in the seminary was for meditation, and I have tried to preserve this habit. Even with the luxury of a cup of coffee (forbidden in the seminary), I am not so awake that I want to babble. No, I want to be quiet, pull myself together after the chaos of my dreams of the night, the energetic getting-ready of my dreams of the morning. I want simply to place myself before the Whole of it and be settled, enlightened, comforted.

I suppose this desire amounts to a wish to be oriented. Facing the east, whence cometh my hopes for a beautiful light that would bring the day alive with God's splendor, I beg direction, ordering, a sense of getting back on the track. Reflecting over what I have to do this day, I try to face the hopes and fears simmering beneath my surface, so come to grips with them that I can muster the self-control I am likely to need. The quiet makes it possible to do this in the presence of God.

In the best of mornings my troubles and distractions run their course and then yield to a silent immensity. Things simplify, empty, get back to basics. I am now more than halfway through my life's span, by most of the actuarial tables. I feel fine, but that only shocks me with a sense of how quickly a human life passes. At the point where I now am it is unclear what my achievement or consequence will be, but it's growing more likely all the time that at the end it will be quite modest. That's the bittersweet likelihood, a simple fact I keep turning over, this way and that, like a lozenge I don't wholly like but have become slightly addicted to.

So my "orientation," which begins with a "What's on the agenda today?" mentality, often is focusing on much less occasional, much more perennial matters by the end. I love to scrape along the bottom, thinking that I'm working on foundational thoughts. When the Spirit is palpable and I feel unusually unthreatened, I love to drop thinking altogether, simply abide and love without words. Now and then I even ask what God wants, how Christ would signify, whether there is something I ought radically to change. I do this timidly, *sotto voce,* quickly, hoping I'm not taken seriously. But now and then it does strike me that God's is the agenda that matters, my judgments of how things are going are of little account. Now and then I read or see something that for a moment takes me to the desert. There outer bleakness and inner unfamiliarity remind me how much in my ordinary day is confected, artificial, arbitrary. This, too, suggests that my self-satisfactions may be worthless, my sense of the possible quite anemic. On the mornings that I get to this point, the Spirit reminds me that Christian life requires ongoing conversion.

My most recent stimulus to this kind of reorientation came from one of the films of the *Long Search* series on world religions. I have been teaching a course on comparative religion with my wife. She uses these films regularly, so she had seen the one on Roman Catholicism and I had not. I therefore was not prepared for the juxtaposition of scenes of St. Peter's, Rome, the pope, and the pageantry with scenes of a Spanish desert, where novices of a small religious order called the Little Brothers of Jesus spend days, weeks, sometimes even a year in absolute solitude. The scenes of the chapel that the Little Brothers have carved in the mountain rock, with the desert stretching below and a vigil light flickering on a rough altar within, were so much more basic and powerful than the scenes of pageantry that I felt my soul tip over. *The judgments of the desert,* I thought, *are much more likely to be the judgments of God than the judgments occurring in St. Peter's.* The lonely novice is in all likelihood much closer to the heart of the Christian matter than the professor who is soon expected to explain the novice's search to the class.

## Self-awareness through the Day

The advantage of visiting the desert is that it orients our perspective and priorities. Like the sea and the mountains, the desert reminds us of who made the world. In the city we can think that we've made the world: the cement, the cables, the smog. City dwellers like me tend to think that food grows in supermarkets. Our instinct is to feel that human interchanges are primary, natural processes are secondary. Easily indeed do we forget the motions of the stars, the pull of the tides, the shifting of the continents. The intense interactions of work and family life narrow our focus to the here and now, the cerebral and emotional rivets that weld "society" and "history." So our self-awareness is quick and constant but superficial. Using the so many other people whom we met throughout the day as mirrors, we get almost too many partial, odd-angled glimpses of ourselves. This can make us much more a persona, an outer mask, than a self of solid substance.

The deserted, vacated times of early morning, late evening, and sabbath can restore balance to our quests for self-knowledge and wise perspective. In the presence of God my persona is unacceptable, what the human mirrors have been saying is secondary. The awareness that dominates Christian quiet is the awareness of the infinite God, the depthless Spirit. Paradoxically enough, this awareness helps me find myself by losing my persona. I become less interested in how I look, how I sound, what impression I make. I become more interested in dealing with ultimate, important things unselfconsciously, egolessly. Probably we only lose all egocentricity when they lower us into the grave, but we can certainly progress beyond adolescence, when the social self we are forming can dwarf all other concerns.

Loving selflessness, monks like the Japanese Buddhist Saigyō have pondered the advantages that sub-human nature has in God's scheme of things. Saigyō (who would have spoken of Buddhanature or Nirvana rather than God) made poetic the rather widespread East Asian instinct that nature's not having to strive for its perfection makes it in some ways superior to human beings.[1] We are usually divided, alienated, partial. Trees, rocks, and rabbits are what they are, do what they do, with little fuss, virtually no slip between spoon and mouth. Because Buddhists and other (yogic) meditators have found egolessness peaceful, even joyous and filled with dazzling light, they have used nature as a luring symbol. Thus in a hallowed shrine such as the Zen Rock Garden in Kyoto one can contemplate rough, angular rocks rising out of a bed of bare, raked sand. The sand represents the emptiness of reality as a whole. The rocks are particulars that become more vivid for being seen against the uncluttered background of the whole. The lesson is that individuals seem more real, are more fully themselves, when we place them against the clean, clearly perceived backdrop of the whole. Remove the clutter of distractions, emotions, other beings half-perceived and individual entities become wonderful, arresting, a key to the interlocked patterns of all beings. Most of the clutter that keeps us from this enlightened view is egocentric, the phantasmagoria of desire.

So Buddhists try to rout desire, and Christians apply themselves to parallel asceticisms. The self-awareness that we try to cultivate through the day is emptying, peacemaking. In the spirit of John the Baptist's "I must decrease, he must increase," Christians trying to put the fruits of their meditations into practice seek to retain some of the recollection of their early mornings, some of the humility of their late nights. The demands of other people are no longer a burden but a chance to wait, attend, listen carefully, keep our own emotions unswirled, our own interests back-burnered. Work can also be viewed as an objective partner with needs to be met, rights to be honored. Out of East Asia's concern for selflessness have come wonderful parables of how to work purely, how losing self-concern can be gaining artful grace. Out of Christian meditations have come similarly rich yields: ministers with eyes cleansed to see their neighbors' needs, scientists more detached, craftsmen more fluent.

Thomas Merton, an influential Christian contemplative, discovered East Asian selflessness in the middle of his monastic career and quickly took it to heart. Translating some of the quirky, poetic thoughts of the early Chinese philosopher Chuang Tzu, Merton recorded the reflections of a butcher who had become selfless:

> There are spaces in the joints; the blade is thin and keen: When this thinness finds that space, there is all the room you need! It goes like a breeze! Hence I have this cleaver nineteen years as if newly sharpened. True, there are sometimes tough joints. I feel them coming, I slow down, I watch closely, hold back, barely move the blade, and whump! the part falls away landing like a clod of earth. Then I withdraw the blade, I stand still, and let the joy of the work sink in.[2]

The joy of the work sinks in when we move self-concern out of the way and give the work access to our depths. The joy of the religious life sinks in when we move self-concern out of the way and give the Mystery access to our depths. Then through the day both the work and the Mystery help us stay aware of how things really hang together, what is really apt to bear service to others and bring peace to ourselves. Then we keep something of our orientation from sunrise, are able to glide rather than lumber.

## The Thread of Feelings

When our self-awareness is self-concern or ego-centricity, we easily feel anxious or vain. When our self-awareness paints us small and on the decrease, unprofitable but blessed servants, we easily feel peaceful and humorous. Our feelings, then, can tip us off to our self-perceptions. Looking back over the day, we may see them as markings through the forest, notches on the trees. There was the anxiety I felt coming into the office after having been out with the flu, knowing I looked hollow-eyed and pasty. There was the surge of smugness and vanity when I read the sales reports and again found myself at the top. Fortunately, there also was the laughter these follies provoked and my letting go of them. Anxiety and vanity have been with me so long that we know one another through and through. They never fail to get in good shots, but I've learned to roll with them and counter with self-deprecating humor. Ah yes, the handsome devil who catches every eye, how will he fare today after his descent to the flu-y depths? The silver-tongued salesman whom none can resist, has he finally set achievements impossible to top?

The feelings that predominate, when faith shapes our consciences, are peace, joy, and perhaps a trace of sadness or poignancy. The peace and joy token the presence and support of the Advocate. When the Spirit abides in a person's heart, that person has the essentials of human fulfillment. The gifts of the Spirit (the consequences of the Advocate's presence) detail this fulfillment: joy, peace, patience, love, and the rest. But the core of the fulfillment is ineffable, something no words can render. Not that the presence of the Spirit, the life of grace, is always mystical rapture, ecstatic bliss. Often it is very commonplace, even dry, dull, or plodding. But under the plodding, or even under sufferings, a certain rightness or integrity endures. If pressed we would have to say that there is no other basic option we could make. In our heart of hearts, we have placed our money on Jesus' God and find it possible to await the outcome patiently, hopefully.

When we become accustomed to discerning the patterns of our feelings, making a check of what beads are assembling on the thread of our days, it becomes possible to distinguish the big, important emotions from the little, lesser ones. Most of our anxieties and vanities are little fellows, best dealt with with a flick of the wrist, the dismissal of humor. Our bedrock peace and joy (final contentment, ability to sleep, capacities to love and to work) are big fellows, supremely important. Discouragement, hopelessness, and deep-seeping bitterness are also big fellows, because they threaten our bedrock peace and joy. If the peace and joy come from openness to the Spirit, the surrounding Mystery of God, the discouragement and hopelessness usually come from closing in on ourselves, or refusing to see external events in the perspective of their ultimate Mystery.

The more regularly we can touch base with the big picture, the deep Mystery, the supportive Spirit, the better able we are to deal with discouragement and hopelessness. We little creatures do not finally matter very much in the perspective of the galaxies. Our worth and significance are better left to God than promoted by ourselves. How the sufferings of innocent people will be redressed is God's business. Our part is to redress the evils we can, defend the innocent we can, and keep pointing to the mystery of goodness, the gratuitous surges of beauty and love.

As middling emotions I would count anger and amusement or irony. Anger is a help against evil but a tool hard to control. The pattern I find in myself is a fairly patient suffering of little wrongs—inefficiencies, nastinesses, lazinesses—and then a flame of hot anger. My emotions build up steam quietly, without my realizing it, and then leap a gap to fierce denunciation. Almost always the people on the receiving end are startled. They have a back-of-the-hand coming, but they never expect this karate blitz. I find it hard not to rage out of control. So I'm almost always sorry in the aftermath and perplexed about my hair trigger. The best defense against its firing seems to be to stay far away from it, realize much earlier where my irritations are leading.

Amusement is a more positive thing, an outcrop of joy and often a gift to others. When I am not grim about life, see myself small and proper, I find many things amusing. The play of little kids is hilarious. The pomps and circumstances of adults are cause of endless giggles. An incongruity here, a pratfall there, and the day takes its place in the unfolding of the divine comedy. Remembering the Old Testament, I sense irony in dozens of human situations. Pot after pot calls kettle black. Glasshousers here, there, and everywhere wind up and pitch their stones. The trace of sadness or poignancy that comes when I think of what might be, what should be, is a balancing reminder of pilgrimage. We have here no lasting city. What we could be will only appear when we know as we are known, see face-to-face.

## The Discipline of Quieting

We best discern the pattern of our emotions when we quiet down, recollect, regain clear waters. As the frenzy on the left and the frenzy on the right testify eloquently, such quieting is not automatic. To become judicious and discerning we must make ourselves quiet, impose some discipline. From the many ways this can be learned I would single out study and church prayer as helps that ought to be nearly automatic in our upbringing. If we have received them, we have something to build upon in private. If we haven't received them, our task is more difficult but by no means impossible.

Having taught in colleges and universities for more than twenty years, I feel qualified to report that good students usually have learned the discipline of quieting. The separation of good students from bad often occurs when professors turn up the burners and start to demand mastery of sizeable chunks of material. Few students below genius caliber can accomplish this without disciplining themselves to put in large chunks of intense, well-focused time. To be sure, good teaching and intrinsically interesting materials can make study bearable, even rewarding or exciting. But nothing can supply for placing one's derrière on the chair, opening the book, and entering the world to be mastered. Students who think otherwise never amount to much, and professors who let students get by thinking otherwise badly disserve their vocation. Half the problems with American education would vanish if teachers and parents would cooperate to enforce this message, especially in high school.

The situation is not so dramatically better in the churches that they have grounds for high pride. The number of American Christian churches teaching their people reflectiveness, quiet, meditation or contemplation to any depth is but a fraction of the whole tally. In the days when I regularly presided at Christian liturgies I found myself building into the design of the worship service small patches of silence. They had to be smaller than I would have liked, for all the practical reasons one can imagine, but even three or four minutes caused squirming and complaining. My goal in insisting on these contemplative patches was not, I hope, sheer perversity. It was to give the word of God space in which to echo, room in which to fill out. Good liturgical prayer is first of all *prayer:* worship, minds and hearts lifted to God. It should be slow (but not draggy), reverent (but not cold), beautiful (but not affected). It should inculcate as well as draw upon quiet and recollection. After a full year of my silences, most of the congregation at least tolerated them, and some actually looked forward to them. Many agreed that scriptural words read out into an expectant quiet resonated with special force. Many assented that a psalm set forth into slow, quiet music floated like a lovely leaf down a sparkling stream. They were people of goodwill, people often led by the Spirit. So they learned that quiet is as much their birthright as noise, silence as splendid a work of God as speech.

I lament the fact that so many people in our culture know only the worlds of noise and speech, are strangers, even foreigners, to the worlds of quiet and silence. By both prejudice and observation, I think that this lack makes such people less human than they might be, less peaceful and joyous. It is true, of course, that the final measure of the Christian life is love. It is true that the noisy mechanic or the talkative babbler who loves God with whole heart and sacrifices for neighbor is more pleasing to the Father of Lights than a silent and arrogant professor. But surely our ideals move us beyond either/or, simplistic dichotomies. Surely the mechanic has a soul reachable by Mozart, the professor better potentialities than isolation and arrogance. The grace of God has a nisus, a thrust, to make us whole and lovely. It is a love that heals and perfects human nature, rounding out the image of God that we might be. When we acquire the disciplines of study and prayer, we offer the Spirit better material for molding. When we add the interior world to our inventory of riches, we are fuller versions of the self foreseen when first God breathed life in us in the womb.

Suppose, though, that our schooling and churching have not been much help, so that we come to adulthood, maybe even middle age, with little love of silence. Suppose we flee from quiet whenever it threatens, call ourselves "people persons" and disparage all monkery. Well, one place where we might grope for a contemplative handle is the most beautiful or significant experience we've lately had. Take the most arresting picture you've seen lately, whether in a museum or out in nature. Try to recall the emotions it evoked, the wonder and inner hushing. Yes, you may well have wanted to cry out, clash your cymbals, shout to your friend. But can you not also recall an invitation to hold yourself still, be present to the show, render it complete attention? Did the Rembrandt or Florida sunset not seem so special that it had a *right* to attention, appreciation, absorption? Would it not have been a lie or slight or piece of bad manners to have run off or rattled on? So too with the Mystery of God, whenever it flashes forth. Whether perceived in nature, or the soul of another person, or the dark of one's own self, the Mystery of God, too, deserves our disciplined attention, has a right to the quiet necessary if we are fully to adore.

## Settling Accounts Late at Night

Orientation in the morning (increasingly selfless) and self-awareness through the day—following the thread of feelings and imposing a disciplined inner quiet— amount to a daily program for developing reflection. From the pole of gentle, holistic reflection at daybreak, I try to swing through the day with sufficient lightness and grace to work usefully, servingly, present to others but mindful of the impulses the Spirit offered at dawn. Other people may have different metabolisms and so need a different model or framework. Those who only wake up at noon and are most thoughtful at four will have to periodize their rhythms accordingly. For me the late afternoon is the butt end of the day, when I feel depressed and prone to mistakes. If possible I fling myself in the hammock and return to the womb. By the time I have awakened, put icy water on my neck, and ingested an evening meal, the concept of God again seems credible, human beings are not all fools or knaves. There comes a rebound of energy and wit; the night beckons and I want to sally forth.

Most nights I only sally forth in my head, my body at the workdesk. Thanks to Thomas Edison, I can try to turn the psychology of the night and the campfire to creative account. Whereas my Hibernian forebears probably sat by a bog telling tall tales that wafted in on the peat smoke, I tell short tales that form into textbooks and tracts. The night, like the before-dawn, is capacious for the imagination. Offering less to the external senses, the night favors memory and fantasy. So I read in leisurely fashion, stopping when something invites me to pause or probe. Then I mount to my loft and try to chart the dances the fairies are purling, their spins and pirouettes. Like the maverick scientists who suggest that nature may be hospitable to almost any questions if we ask them sincerely, I find that the thought-realities I handle dance somewhat as I pipe. Of course there are regularities to the Christian ballet. Certain steps, intervals, and tones have to sound. But the Word's having taken flesh means that all of material reality is instinct with spirit, full of the meaning it groans to bring forth.

With time I have found theology coming closer to poetry, icon and metaphor merging. God, the great silence from which all expressions come, to which all expressions return, is as fresh and new as our best minds' mintings. With Jesus to anchor their *economy* (a word the early Fathers loved), our exchanges with theological reality mainly become permissible probes, like the pawings and sniffings of frisky kittens. What turns out hateful, hurtful, or evil of course becomes forbidden. But real sin is seldom playful, since real sin is not the breaking of laws, the skirting of rules, but the freezing of the heart, the refusal to love, couple, and create.

When my brain has teemed enough and I've edited out the worst licenses, the true end of the day comes in sight. By the stars that twinkle over the sunspace, or the soft notes of peaceable composers, my spirit tries to simplify and return to home base. There it sifts things out, makes columns of assets and liabilities, presses down a seal of red wax. This is not legalism, bureaucracy, or works-righteousness. My accounts are always too unimpressive for that. I never accomplish all that I hoped I would, seldom find much to take pride in. Almost always, though, I find moments to cheer, images to store, reasons for thanksgiving. Today, for instance, Sally (her real name) sallied in to return some books. She was wearing little red sneakers. Since Sally is nothing if not chic, sneakers must now be fashion, but they struck my funny bone. Thus they were bound to enter some collage I would construct, bound soon to be summoned and processed. *How nice,* I thought, *to have a work that can process experience so directly.* Religious writing is a poor, derivative art, yet art it can be nonetheless. Like the painter who sees a ribbon in a little girl's hair and has to use just that hue, or the composer who hears a peasant tune and must weave it into his quartet, I work in, factor from, construct with the sights and sounds of my days. In this way I keep faith with and exemplify the central truth of all Christian spirituality—that God comes concretely, in the experiences of everyday.

Thus usually the accounts turn over and by grace show a profit. God forgives the debits, shakes the messes around, and, like an African basket diviner, reads meaning out of the scraps. Today it was red sneakers (and the unwonted experience of someone actually returning borrowed books). Tomorrow it may be the Malaysian dances our foreign students are putting on, or something I don't even suspect right now.

Blessed are the nights we retire anticipating the morrow, thinking it may bring good surprise. Paul believed that where sin (negativity of all sorts) abounds, grace abounds the more. What is the justification for so bold a faith? Where does Paul get his nerve? From remembering the resurrection of Jesus, reflecting again on time's center. Dying, Christ destroyed our death; rising, he restored our life; living in our midst, he makes all our accounts favorable.

# 4.

# CASES AND CRITERIA

*A Problem at Work*

We have been dealing with consciousness and conscience, trying to describe the interior world from which our insights, judgments, and decisions emanate. Our central notion has been reflection: the unique ability of the human species to bend back on itself, be both subject and object of an inquiry. In the depths of the reflective self lie some of the most pregnant wonders of religion and faith. Visiting those depths morning and evening can polarize our time usefully, maturingly. It can begin to emerge that a Christian conscience is but a moral awareness informed by Christ's Spirit. What we do in trying to live out our faith is not dictated by a set of external codes but guided, tutored by the Spirit of Jesus. The love of this Spirit, poured forth in our hearts, is the energy of a genuinely Christian ethics. The instincts developed by this Spirit mean more than a hundred sermons or books. It is good for our minds to study, especially when they go slowly and ponderingly, but it is better for our hearts to pray. As Thomas à Kempis saw, it is good to know the definition of compunction, but better by far to feel compunction in one's heart.

Let us therefore move to some concrete cases that might illustrate how the Christian conscience we have been describing might feel in actual life. The first case comes from the world of work, where many of us spend almost a third of our adult lives. Once, in a galaxy not so far away, a husband and wife were invited to go east to find their fortune. The smooth salesman said they would have a nonpareil chance to share 1.5 jobs and arrange their days flexibly. The notion of shared work was new to the company that was hiring, but the chance to obtain a highly trained husband-wife team was intriguing to the boss. So the couple packed up their kids, their belongings, and their beagle and started traveling against the sun.

When they arrived on the new scene and became acquainted with their jobs, it was distressingly clear that the salesman had spoken half-truths. They would have 1.5 positions, but not as the two .75's he had promised. No, the man would be 1.0 and regular, the woman would be .5 and part-time (with large disadvantages in fringe benefits and general status). Also, while it was true that the boss was enthusiastic about the new package, the boss's inner council of senior employees was vehemently opposed. This opposition had little to do with the couple themselves, a lot to do with long-term office warfare. But the bottom line, as the seniors made chillingly clear, was that the couple would never be welcome, were in for a constant series of ambushes and snipes. So they knew in their bones the place had no future. They had moved two thousand miles and fallen further behind.

The crisis came when new work assignments were announced at a staff meeting. The woman, especially, found none of her interests honored, all of her initiatives bypassed. When the man inquired how the assignments came about, he was told the senior council had worked them out. Half-aware of what he was doing, he looked at the council leader and said: "Fine. Then let the senior council change them. This is the grossest self-service I've seen in a long time. You bozos have simply feathered your own nests. A cretin couldn't think these assignments bore any resemblance to fairness, but tell me your justification." The silence was deafening. The only faces that did not blush were those already turned to stone. The couple got better work assignments, but they could hear the gate slamming. Sure enough, at the earliest opportunity the senior members (who by then had forced out the old boss) welched on the implications of the couple's contract and gave them the gate. In the time between the announcement and the actual termination, the couple did little else besides ponder what had happened. Had they stood up for principle at the cost of realism? Had they stood up for principle at all, or just given vent to frustration? What sufferance of mismanagement and injustice is part of most people's necessity? When is a work situation intolerable?

These questions are not easy to answer. Many factors weigh in the balance. For this couple, job security would have meant the wherewithal to enjoy their kids and develop themselves culturally. Still, if such security meant day after day of oppressive work its price was dubiously high. In fact, the woman already had felt her self-esteem and professional confidence oozing away. The man had discovered he would not take patronizing abuse, especially from "superiors" he judged worthless. So while the time until they secured another job was troubled and anxious, the couple found little in their leaving itself to lament. They had come to the job in good faith, put up with initial injustices and maltreatments, and only become obstreperous when pushed to their limits. Their humiliation at being judged and dismissed by inferiors, seniors superior only in age, taught them volumes about the psychological damages of the oppressed, the internalizations to which all the degraded are prone. Six months after they were in their new work situation the woman woke up one morning, poked her sleepy husband, and announced that she finally felt free.

For the couple who had gone east, the postmortems in which they reviewed their decision and what had happened to them brought a greater appreciation of freedom from oppression on the job. As well, they brought the realization that it is not good to seal one's fate by an unplanned, emotional outburst. Like many of us, they botched their first try at mediating a conflicted, no-win situation. They only emerged wiser by having suffered. Trial and error is as much the rule in the moral life as in any other. God does not give us prescience, by which we might foresee all eventualities. God only asks that we do our best and learn from the consequences. Wise people are not people who have made no mistakes. Wise people are people who have profited from their mistakes, made sure they did their best not to repeat them. God is a Father whose children are allowed the freedom to make mistakes. Like the father of the prodigal son in Luke 15, God knows that freedom is the condition of both growth and genuine love. God's grace is the promise that we will always be welcomed back, that God will always come more than halfway. As soon as we repent, recover from our mistakes, or ask to return to the light, we see God coming to greet us.

## A Problem with a Child

Picture another couple, somewhat older than the first, with a cluster of teenagers. The parents are happy enough in their work, but their work is neither so secure nor so profitable that they can attend to the needs of their children with wholly free minds. Perhaps as a result, the middle child is going through a patch of rebelliousness, disobeying as a way to assert or find herself. The parents are grateful she is getting by in school, avoiding drugs and other big problems, but her negativity troubles their sleep. They don't understand what they are doing wrong, why she has turned so nasty. Neither gentle talks nor stern commands seem to work. She is too old to spank and, apparently, too immature to reason with.

One night the daughter comes home two hours beyond her curfew. The parents have started to worry, so they berate her for not having called. She dismisses their upset and anger with a superior air, telling them she can't be bothered with such trivia. That is the final flame to their tinder and they ground her indefinitely. This gives them no joy, for they are not vindictive people. It seems to give her no cause to rethink her behavior. The situation is stalemated until, after several weeks, the parents again try to talk things through with her. Going out for a special Sunday brunch, they try in their most reasonable manner to explain why her behavior so upset them, what goes through parents' minds when it reaches 2:00 A.M. and no daughter has appeared.

"Suppose," they say, "we had gone off to the shore and left you at home in charge of Brian. You told Brian to be back from Jimmy's house by 10:00 P.M. and he had not arrived by 12:00. How would you feel? Wouldn't you start to worry? You know that the road between our house and Jimmy's is dark and that cars race along it. Wouldn't you have wondered about an accident? Wouldn't you have called Jimmy's by 10:30, and if no one had answered [as had happened when the parents had tried to reach where the daughter was supposed to be] wouldn't your fears have been compounded?"

The daughter had to admit that probably she would have had thoughts like that (although she was sure she wouldn't have "freaked out" the way her parents had). She could see there had been some justification for their reaction. But then she surprised them by saying, "Really, though, you know, I was just trying to see what would happen. I mean, I don't feel like a little kid anymore. I feel I should be able to decide whether or not to go with the other kids to get a pizza or drag Douglas, even if it's midnight. After all, I'm sixteen years old. Women used to have two or three kids by the time they were sixteen years old. Sixteen-year-olds have won the U.S. Open in tennis and swum the English Channel. And I have to check in like a baby, can hardly move off my own block."

So the three brunchers picked at their eggs, sipped at their coffee, and worked out a compromise. The daughter would get more freedom, provided she kept her parents informed (called in). She would get a vote of confidence that she could handle herself, would use her head and not get into dangerous or compromising situations. She would also get more responsibility: demands that she get better grades in school, do more of the housework, and chauffeur Brian to some meetings and practices. It was a tentative arrangement, worked out on a trial basis, with suspicion and hesitation on both sides. But the daughter seemed to hold herself straighter and the parents let go of some of their frustration.

When the parents discussed it later, the mother reflected, half to herself: "Well, some of what she says is true enough. At other times sixteen-year-olds have been full adults. I think our culture retards kids' maturation too much to consider sixteen adult today, but probably some kids start making the changeover then. The fact that Peter [the eldest child] didn't rebel the way Lisa has may just say that these two kids are different. Boys do mature more slowly. Lisa may well feel more frustrated, have more need to break out. Let's give it a try, Ned. Let's let her fail before we say she can't handle more freedom. She didn't use to be imprudent or wild. Maybe if she doesn't feel hemmed in she'll show she can be levelheaded." To date, it has worked out well. Given a clear chance to behave like an adult, Lisa has come through with flying colors.

Lisa's parents had to make their decision to change their treatment of her flying by the seat of their pants. Not only had they never had a sixteen-year-old daughter before, even if they had this case probably would have been different from anything they had previously seen. In flying by the seat of one's pants, "feel" is all important. Until we can sketch a scenario that seems fitting, feels good, we're uneasy and don't have peace. The parents knew that their basic reaction was sound, but they wanted to hear Lisa's side. When she showed signs of understanding their worry, it seemed possible she might be growing up. Then it was easier to grasp her frustrations, see where she might need more latitude. What had been an antagonistic or adversarial situation started to become cooperative. A certain "contractual" agreement emerged, with duties that balanced rights. If Lisa were going to be treated as an adult in terms of late night hours she would have to perform as an adult in terms of schoolwork, housework, and helping out with her younger brother. When she agreed to this contract and began fulfilling her part, the parents could feel they'd made a good decision. Prior to her actual performance, however, they had to content themselves with feeling the bargain made sense.

The crux of many conscientious decisions is how they feel at core. If we suffer no troubling doubts, rest unagitated, we can accept the judgment that there are no further questions and put the decision into gear. It may turn out that we've made a mistake; that is always possible. But we need not, should not, second-guess ourselves, read into the past knowledge we only gained later. Of course, we should study the mechanics of what turn out to be bad decisions. Perhaps we made unwarranted assumptions or prematurely closed off other possibilities. Next time we should make sure we don't repeat those failings. But if we acted in good conscience, without big doubts at the time, we ought to let what was done be done, leave the past to God.

## A Problem with God

This acceptance of human fallibility, and our related need frequently to give over an imperfect past to God, leads to the third case I offer. In retrospect, it seems a case of commonplace depression. At the time claims were made that it was a case of loss of faith in God.

A woman apparently blessed in her family life and happy in her work found herself feeling unworthy to receive communion, out of place in the house of God. When, during counseling, she probed these feelings, she found that she resented being supposed to be grateful for her good marriage, supposed to feel blessed in her job. Yes, her marriage was better than many, her job brought satisfactions. But five kids were a heavy burden, an engineer husband was not a complete boon.

Running her house took more energy and patience than most people realized. If she were a man her job would have been paying her a third more and she would have had fine prospects for promotion. For several years these frustrations had been clustering together and gathering steam. She hated having to go to a church of smiley people who never would understand such things. She hated having a God at whom she could never shake her fist. She had learned in childhood that serene was God and serene she'd better be. She couldn't stand God, and she certainly didn't feel right about receiving him.

By the time she had talked things out to this degree of clarity, the woman knew half her problem and solution. It took some ministerial authority to convince her that her image of God was unbiblical, Abraham and Job were great shakers of fists. But the clincher came on her own, when she took up Luke 7:36–50. There the notion that Jesus forgave sinners became vivid and affecting. The woman who wiped Jesus' feet with her hair and tears, who was praised for her great love (which came from the forgiveness of her great sin), captured the troubled mother's heart. She had no difficulty seeing this Magdalene as real, human, someone God might well have decided to re-create. The sinful woman had not been perfect, gotten her act together, and then felt God's grace. No, she had been pardoned while in her sins, when first she desired to change. The counselee could honestly say that *she* desired to change, wanted to be rid of her anger. She could honestly say she didn't need a perfectionist God, let alone a perfectionist self. Her kids were dear, her husband fine, her job a great satisfaction. If it were legitimate to blow off steam, go public with frustration, she would have very little doubt she couldn't handle.

When the counselor suggested going public by humor—satirizing her kids' clutter, her husband's precision, the sexism she found on the job—he gave the woman the escape valve she'd needed. When he moved on to suggest a prayer that might satirize her old notion of God (playing before a crotchety old man, tugging his beard, and telling him to loosen up), the woman felt icebergs of resentment loosen. She went out and found a new church, where people didn't have always to be upbeat, where God could take a little flak. She talked things out with her kids, her husband, and her boss—humorously, ironically. Now she's a warm and strong lady, deeper than before her crisis. Having broken through crusts of false conscience, she knows a strong joy and peace.

## *The Christian Fruits by Which to Know*

The woman who redecorated her psyche, changing her image of God and giving herself new stripes of humor, emerged from her depression or crisis with a shot of energy. Once again she felt life surge through her veins, enthusiasm put pep in her step. The crabbed notion of God she'd been suffering gave way to a God who forgives. The ladylike portrait she'd been trying to match gave way to a sturdy fist shaker. In interesting tandem, her God and her self became much more real, much more likable.

Realism, likableness, energy, and similar signs of life are hard to achieve when we're wounded. If several of our cylinders are not firing, we find it hard to get up to speed. Often we don't realize the handicaps under which we've been operating until they've been removed. For the woman alienated from God, it took counseling and a special insight into an apposite passage of scripture. Frequently counseling or spiritual direction is the religious equivalent of a visit to the doctor: diagnosis and medication to fight the virus that's been weakening us. Other times it is like the tune-up that resets our car's timing, restores its good mileage. A skillful spiritual director can sharpen our perceptions of how our religious life likely is unfolding, what an honest opening to God likely is requiring. When spiritual direction is kindly, humane, offered by people who make it clear that they are but fellow pilgrims, it can be a great source of comfort.[1] As from an intelligent and sympathetic support group, one comes away feeling one is not alone, other people are struggling with the same problems.

It is not good for people to be alone, scripture counsels, and it is not good for Christians to have a notion of God that makes God distant. Unless God is the vitality surging in our blood when we are most healthy, the desire we feel when we are most passionate, the strength holding our bones when we are most enduring, God is not the living flame of love he wants to be, the nursing mother she has promised she will be.

One of the best literary portrayals of this insight occurs in Alice Walker's *The Color Purple*. In the dialogue between the worldly wise Shug and the long-suffering Celie we see the personal religion that not only has kept Shug going but has given her world a glow:

> Here's the thing, say Shug. The thing I believe. God is inside you and inside everybody else. You come into the world with God. But only them that search for it inside find it. And sometimes it just manifest itself even if you not looking, or don't know what you looking for.

According to Shug, trouble causes (or enables) most of us to see It. Celie is puzzled.

> It? I ast.
> Yeah, It. God ain't a he or a she, but a It.
> But what do it look like? I ast.
> Don't look like nothing, she say. It ain't a picture show. It ain't something you can look at apart from anything else, including yourself. I believe God is everything, say Shug. Everything that is or ever was or ever will be. And when you can feel that, and be happy to feel that, you've found It.
> Shug a beautiful something, let me tell you. She frown a little, look out cross the yard, lean back in her chair, look like a big rose.
> She say, My first step from the old white man was trees. Then air. Then birds. Then other people. But one day when I was sitting quiet and feeling like a motherless child, which I was, it come to me: that feeling of being part of everything, not separate at all. I knew that if I cut a tree, my arm would bleed. And I laughed and I cried and I run all around the house. I knew just what it was. In fact, when it happen, you can't miss it.

Shug goes on to say that all of our feelings, even sexual feelings, are part of God's plan—created by God and loved by God.

> God love all them feelings. That's some of the best stuff God did. And when you know God loves 'em you enjoys 'em a lot more. You can just relax, go with everything that's going, and praise God by liking what you like.
> God don't think it dirty? I ast.
> Naw, she say. God made it. Listen, God love everything you love—and a mess of stuff you don't. But more than anything else, God love admiration.
> You saying God vain? I ast.
> Naw, she say. Not vain, just wanting to share a good thing.

Shug is sure that it makes God mad "if you walk by the color purple in a field somewhere and don't notice it." Celie wonders what happens when God is mad and Shug responds:

> Oh, it make something else. People think pleasing God is all God care about. But any fool living in the world can see it always trying to please us back.
> Yeah? I say.
> Yeah, she say. It always making little surprises and springing them on us when us least expect.
> You mean it want to be loved, just like the bible say.
> Yes, Celie, she say. Everything want to be loved. Us sing and dance, make faces and give flower bouquets, trying to be loved.[2]

## Love and Do What You Will

When the spiritual masters discuss the discernment of spirits, telling us that peace and joy are the hallmarks of the good Spirit's workings in people of faith, they give invaluable testimony. Nonetheless, like all testimony, it must be interpreted, and it is possible to interpret "peace and joy" in a pallid, antiseptic fashion. Testimony such as Shug's can protect against such a tendency, reminding us that the pious has no special rights over-against the earthy. The intense and passionate can be as godly as the serene and detached. The Christian God, maker of heaven and earth, is available in every creature, every honest emotion, every part of human living that is real. Thus when Paul started signing off to the Philippians he wrote:

> Rejoice in the Lord always; again I will say, Rejoice. Let all men know your forbearance. The Lord is at hand. Have no anxiety about anything, but in everything by prayer and supplication with thanksgiving let your requests be made known to God. And the peace of God, which passes all understanding, will keep your hearts and your minds in Christ Jesus. Finally, brethren, whatever is true, whatever is honorable, whatever is just, whatever is pure, whatever is lovely, whatever is gracious, if there is any excellence, if there is anything worthy of praise, think about these things. What you have learned and received and heard and seen in me, do; and the God of peace will be with you.
>
> —Philippians 4:4–9

Paul clearly sensed that to the pure—or even those only aspiring to be pure—all things are pure. When our centers rest in the Spirit, are concentric with God, nothing need separate us from the love of God. This does not mean proclaiming ourselves high saints. It has nothing to do with human pride or self-satisfaction. It has to do only with God's grace, God's priority, God's sufficiency. In all things natural, God is like a painter or craftsman soliciting our admiration. In all things human, God is like a lover, wanting to please, open up deeper and deeper realms for sharing. The conscience of the person given over to God therefore overflows now and then with a universal love. The peace and joy that wave forth when one is carried by the Spirit would embrace all tribes and nations. On our own we do indeed remain pocked and pitted. The snakes and toads of unruly passion, the stupidities and twists of unruly self-love, continue to darken our psyches. But they are tamed, shunted to the side, because we are not on our own. We have been given the Spirit Helper. God sees us in the lineaments of Christ. Saul, persecuting the church, was knocked from his horse and taught the lesson that the church and Christ are one. John, meditating deeply on the new life that entered the world when the Word took flesh, set believers in a relation to Christ as organic as the branches in the vine.

The best sorts of actions take place when they are empowered by the divine love and grace. Out of the fullness of the heart the mouth speaks; out of the dispositions of the heart the whole person acts. Let the heart, the center of the self, rest in the Spirit, the "Proceeding Love" of the Trinity, and the mouth will speak praise of God, the whole person will love neighbor as self. The passionate God, as Rosemary Haughton's stunning book of that name makes plain, is alive in all our pain and joy making the world new.[3] The more we open to this God, this Mystery we find when we reflect and settle down toward our centers, the more we can serve this God's purposes, be conspirators and collaborators. If we are conspiring with God's Proceeding Love, working with the One in whom all things hold together so that God may be all in all, we cannot be acting unethically, immorally, in ways that violate our consciences. The valid intuition of the philosophers and mystics who have spoken of a plane "beyond good and evil" is the sense that when we are taken up by the Spirit strictly human calculi fade away. Evil is avoided, good is pursued, unthinkingly, "automatically," because the Total Good runs the show, attracts all the attention.

Augustine, perhaps the most passionate of the church fathers, wrote many epigrammatic, memorable lines. None is more germane to our concern in this book, though, than his lapidary ethical summary: "Love and do what you will." In Latin this famous line runs: "Ama et fac quod vis." The stress, therefore, is on making the action flow from the love. Let us but be in love, cling passionately to God, open to the Spirit's ravishments, and what we want will automatically be good, what we shun will automatically be ungodly. The Spirit, the God of love, will be changing our being, remaking our substance. Inevitably our action, our behavior, our ethics will change.

Those who share in the divine nature must express something of divinity. However shallow their share, however weak their hold, they must speak, think, comport themselves as children of God. As analogies one thinks of the legendary changes that come with conversions, fallings in love, parenthoods. The alcoholic long reborn through Alcoholics Anonymous bears little resemblance to the prior drunkard. The wild, reckless youth who finds a good woman or a good God is scarcely recognizable in middle age.[4] The teenager on her way to ruin, cheapening and sliding toward the streets, can be calm and glowing a year later, as she bathes her little child. When we love, what we will to do is the best we can do, the loveliest imaging of God. When we love, what we will approximates God's will, since God is the goodness of utter, infinite love.

# 5.

# THE MOVE TO JUDGMENT

*Reviewing Understanding*

On the way to purifying our loves so that one day we may do as we will, we do well to strengthen our grasp on the procedures of judgment. If genuinely religious affections make us transcend ourselves by taking us to the Mystery of God, and genuinely moral decisions make us transcend ourselves by taking us to what is objectively good, then genuinely truthful judgments make us transcend ourselves by taking us to reality. The issue of a good judgment, in which we have realized that we have the grounds for saying yes or no to a proposition, is a commitment of ourselves to an objective state of affairs. This commitment may have to be qualified, since our data or certitude of understanding may be qualified. But in itself judgment makes us people who take a stand, put ourselves on the line, assert that we are knowers and reality is knowable. From the scientist asserting that an hypothesis has indeed been verified, to a wife asserting that her husband does indeed have a drinking problem, human beings can and do weigh evidence, review interpretations, bring themselves to a judicious calm, and then say yes or no, turn thumbs up or thumbs down.

In any serious matter, the experience of this judgmental review is revealingly maturing. The scientist testing an hypothesis of significance realizes, at least implicitly, that the build of reality is at stake. Nature is sufficiently real or objective to force scientists to try to honor it, render it accurately, describe its patterns as they actually do occur. If nineteenth-century science over-emphasized the supposed objectivity of this interpretational process, tending to picture nature as an inert machine one might disassemble as easily as a steam engine, twentieth-century science has made it clear that nature and the human mind are engaged in a delicate dialogue. Indeed, nature and the human mind seem so coordinated to one another that anything thinkable is worth trying to verify. Still, only when something thinkable has been verified—tested out, corroborated—will the competent scientist proclaim it solid theory, part of the information about the world on which reasonable people may rely.

The scientist of integrity therefore is almost bound to be a judicious, quite mature person. He or she may not always make sufficient allowance for the differences between human realities and natural realities, but the long years of training in dispassion, objectivity, careful observation, and testing will have honed high human skills. Analogously, the spouse or parent of integrity finds many prods to maturity, many calls to become sober and reflective. To continue with the example of the wife passing review on her husband's drinking: Such a review demands paying careful attention to experience (the patterns of the husband's excesses), steeling oneself against unpleasant implications (I have on my hands a person out of control), and starting to face challenging decisions (If Jack is indeed an alcoholic, what am I going to do about it?). We may distinguish the processes of the spouse from the processes of the person in the lab coat, calling the intelligence of one "common sense" and the intelligence of the other "science," but each person is exercising the same human apparatus, entering into the same human interiority. Each is reflecting on experience, passing review on prior hypotheses, and coming to grips with the human capacity and responsibility to deal with reality as it is (in contrast to the way we may wish it were). When we become people who make serious, deep, or hard judgments, we become people who have passed out of the land of adolescence and are now solid citizens of adulthood.

In the beginnings of the judgmental process, we must review our previous understandings. So we may picture the troubled woman (let's call her Mary Sue) pouring herself a second cup of coffee after the kids have thundered out to the school bus and letting the gentle rain quiet her spirit. She has things on her mind, after last night's embarrassing party, and somehow they seem things she should have been dealing with months ago. When she took the keys from Jack, finally admitting to herself that he was too drunk to drive, she crossed a line she had for some time sensed but backed away from. Had she let herself see, she would have found a pattern long ago: the escalation to three or even four drinks before dinner each night; the steady tippling each weekend; the increasingly spotty record of attendance at the kids' games, civic events, even meetings connected with his job. More and more there were times he didn't account for, lame explanations for dates missed. More and more drinking crept into his conversation, his humor, his concept of recreation.

Yes, had she let herself follow up on her uneasinesses, attend to her misgivings, Mary Sue would have found patterns of trouble, storm warnings, months ago. Well, no sense crying over spilt milk. The point now was to be sure of those patterns, come to a firm judgment about their reality and degree of seriousness. If a man got himself so drunk that he could not drive, virtually passed out in the seat beside her, had to be helped up the stairs to bed, was he not obviously in trouble? If this drunkenness represented not a unique, bizarre phenomenon but the culmination of lesser drunkenness he had been exhibiting for several years, did it not signify a strong danger of alcoholism, a pressing need for remedial action? So Mary Sue finishes off her cup of coffee, raps on the rainy pane, and reaches for the phone book. A call to her family doctor, a call to Alcoholics Anonymous, and she is out the door in search of help.

## Checking Bias

Would that all judges were as honest and resolute as Mary Sue. Alas, the unreality that pits so many lives suggests that most of us are far less rational. For fear of what we shall find, we delay our review of experience, our reflective journey to the scenes of our misgivings. For lack of self-knowledge, we fail to note how we twist the data, make patterns that threaten us the less while they distort reality the more. To be a good judge, a person of mature reflective intelligence, most of us must undergo a stripping of bias, an ascesis of willfulness. Until we have reached the point where we honor what is so more than what we would like to be so, we are not masters of our own inner tribunal. And, until then, we cannot be people of mature conscience, because we cannot admit things as they are, the words that the Spirit actually is speaking.

Once I worked with a man who so badly misjudged what I expected of him that he has remained a vivid cautionary example. He seemed a competent scholar so I agreed to collaborate with him on a sizeable project. The arrangement was that he would make a first survey of some options we ought to consider, we would meet to discuss his survey, and then I would put together a proposal to the people who were to fund the project. This seemed clear and firmly agreed, so we parted with the understanding that I could expect his survey within the month. When the month had passed, and no survey had arrived, I called to find out what was happening. Well, he had been delayed, but he hoped to get to the project quite soon. Please do, I said, and please let me know if you find yourself unable to meet your commitments.

Another month went by, no survey showed up, so I called and arranged a luncheon meeting. This began badly because the man came a half hour late (he claimed he had misunderstood the time), and soon it became worse, because he offered no explanation for his nonperformance. When I finally asked him directly he mumbled, "I didn't know you were so precise about dates and things. I just thought, well, we'll get around to it soon enough." At that point I laid out for my "colleague" the precise conditions of our future collaboration. Either he would have the survey to me in one week or I would get another partner. Further, either he would show me the courtesy of keeping me informed of his progress (or, more importantly, of his nonprogress) or he would find his professional reputation in tatters, for I would tell the sponsors of our project he had proven both incompetent and irresponsible.

My point in introducing this example is not to raise issues about personnel management or the politics of collaboration. It is to illustrate the egregious misjudgments, miscalculations, misperceptions of reality that many people regularly commit. There was no way that this man could have seen my track record clearly and come up with the expectation that I would not hold him to what he had said he would do. Nothing in our original discussion gave him any valid reason to expect that our schedule could be treated casually. Yet his self-delusion was such that he overlooked these massive evidences. His bias in favor of *laissez-faire*, go with the flow, left him completely out of touch with the reality in front of him. Because he could not or would not do what he had pledged himself to do, he had to blot out that pledge, forget the partner he had bound himself to work with.

Usually we do not check our biases, oppose the pressures that twist us from the truth, because we cannot face what an unbiased judgment would render. This is the wisdom in the intuition of many kindly people that those who are most irritating and irresponsible probably are those most suffering inner turmoils, self-loathings, or utter lacks of confidence. That they may appear arrogant, proud, overbearing does not gainsay this hypothesis. Their excess of self-assertion likely is but the manic phase of a pulsation in which the depressive phase finds them bereft of self-love. The therapies of the gospel, which offers all people a self-love guaranteed by the love of God, therefore go to the crux of many personality disorders. My only caveat in agreeing that whenever possible we should preach these therapies in all kindness is that this preaching not absolve the recipient of the responsibility to fulfill his or her commitments. What was most shocking to me in my encounter with this scholarly deadbeat was his surprise at being taken to task for his technicolor dereliction of duty. Clearly I was one of the first people who had ever told him that unless he grew up and acted like an adult he would get a painful spanking. His inner furies might have been less fearsome and debilitating had his elders and peers not babied him through the years of his formation.

## Establishing Peace

I hope that the reader will agree with this juxtaposition of love and demand, acceptance and holding to account, because it is axial to the view of conscience that I hold. We all have sinned and fallen short of the glory of God. We all depend on the astounding gratuity that God has loved us first. But this dependence and gratuity ought to enable, encourage, husband our responsibility, not support us in self-indulgence, bias, or irrationality. God the judge is less ultimate than God the loving parent, but something in the symbol of God the "judge" is very important: a respect for the objective order of things, a sensitivity to the moral demands in human exchanges. True enough, those who would make ethics a legalism, perverting God's judgment into inflexible or cruel narrownesses, miss the heart of moral responsibility. It is not the niggling details of a compact that matter but its heart and soul. My erstwhile collaborator was not perverse because he did not deliver what he had promised at the stated day and hour. He was perverse because he did not hoist the basic load he had agreed to, and because he ignored the communication, mutual respect, and empathy that must obtain if human intercourse is to be fruitful at all.

When the love of God crashes through a person's defenses, the self-protections that have been preventing the person from responsible behavior may come tumbling down. This love need not arrive with telegrams and banners announcing its heavenly source. It may wear the humble, much less threatening guise of friendship, romance, or parental affection. But, whatever the mode, its potential effect is enormous. For when the love of God stabilizes our hearts, we need not skitter away, may finally be able to stand and face what is actually occurring, whether we like it or not. And then something of the peace that passes the world's understanding may infiltrate our spirits, letting us (perhaps for the first time) approach the equanimity, the balance of mind and heart, necessary for good, realistic judgments.

Perhaps I can best illustrate this peace, and the process by which it may establish itself, by resurrecting two personages who were influential at an early stage of my professional career. One was a professor emeritus, ripe in years and goodness. In the midst of an agitated department (whose leaders were quite ambivalent about his presence), this senior scientist and theologian went about his daily work with the sweetness of a man well reconciled to reality, the peace of a man who had descended to his depths and emerged fully integral. Again and again, whatever the potential upset, he would proffer words of reason, realism, and hope. Without at all denying the debilitating ways of his fellow human beings, whose pettinesses and shortsightednesses would bring him to physical groans, he would in effect tell us younger colleagues that this was the way things had always been, in every place he'd ever worked, every prior phase of his long career. Some people would spend their time politicking and complaining. Other people would do their work and put their shoulders to the wheel. The politicians would get more benefits than they deserved, bear fewer burdens than was right, but they would never machinate their way to real joy. The solid workers would be penalized in this-worldly terms, not milking the system anywhere near so successfully as their shrewder brothers and sisters, but in another calculus the satisfactions they found in doing solid work, making the enterprises of the whole group go forward, would give them a sustenance, at times even a surprising joy, that would prove far more valuable than all the politicians' passing advantages. Then the professor emeritus would smile his little smile, hang up his teacup, and go back for another stint of productive work.

The contrasting specimen, a man without peace of soul and so without good (balanced and socially useful) judgment, was a strange expatriate scholar who spewed forth bile wherever he went. In flight from an oppressive political regime somewhere back in the Balkans, he was a giant obstacle to hope, progress, sweetness or light of any stamp. On the left he saw only soft-headedness and capitulation to trends that would debilitate scholarly standards, moral probity, the traditions of Western culture. On the right he saw only a willingness to challenge his anger, his overbearing nature, and his own contributions to Western culture that made him label the right fossilized, too stupid to appreciate the revelations coming through Balkany-in-exile. The result would have been comic had the man not eviscerated a dozen projects that bore promise, crushed a dozen tender shoots of collegiality and enthusiasm. Because they were not sure enough of their own souls, peaceful enough at their own depths, most of his fellow workers were not willing to stand up to him. The professor emeritus did yeoman work, but his quiet smile and small still voice often were too subtle or lofty for the majority. So there was considerably less joy in that Mudville than there might have been, considerably more need for younger people like myself to walk the streets late at night and crystallize some personal convictions.

The peace at the center of good judgment, whether it comes as an unprecedented grace or is the crystallization of hard self-questioning, therefore tends to bring a certain sobriety. Without displacing joy and lightheartedness, it reminds the good judge that this world is no lasting city, human perfection should not be expected in one's lifetime. In the twinkling of an eye human beings can muster acts of extraordinary goodness, but they can also turn sour, contrary, or even evil. The elder of my two examples was saying that one should be surprised at human negativity (otherwise one would expect it and so foreclose hope) without being crushed by it. If a particular negativity cannot be ignored, bypassed as trivial, then it must be faced, named, and fought. But, either way, one can still keep a core peace, let go, and leave the final outcome to God.

## Asserting and Deciding

When epistemologists (those who study human knowledge) describe the processes of judgment, they usually report that they must distinguish between the assertions that make a declaration about reality and the decisions that move the declarer into action. The assertions (or negations) ideally are the fruits of the person's having understood that he or she has sufficient reasons for judging a reality to be, or not to be, in such and such a way. If the reality in question were the professor emeritus, and the question were whether or not his counsel was wise, the crux would be what one found in reviewing what he had said and comparing that with what had eventuated. Let him have said, repeatedly and clearly, that politicking would bring no peace, spending time on cabals would prove far less satisfying than doing solid work; let this advice seem verified by one's experience and observation; and one would have sufficient reasons for judging, "Yes, Professor Schilling is a wise man, a counselor I should listen to most respectfully." Let such a pattern of consistent counsel not appear, or appear without clear verification, and one would have to bracket that judgment, hold out for more confirmation. Finally, let such a pattern seem contradicted by the data, so that memory did not find the professor repeatedly giving such advice or evaluation, or did not find such advice proving true or illuminating, and one would have to deny the proposition: "No, Professor Schilling is not a wise man, his counsel is not to be taken to heart."

It is the property of judicious people to be able to make these reviews calmly, accurately, in peace of spirit, and so say their yes or no as the data warrant, without tilt or stain. It is the property of injudicious people not to be able to make such reviews. Because of their inattention or stupidity or bias or intemperance the injudicious are not able to turn their experiences over calmly and accurately, are unwilling or unable to let the chips fall where they may. Since one cannot be wise without judiciousness, the import of being able to assert or deny well is gigantic. One who is not wise does not see things, deal with things, as they are. He or she goes through life like a sleepwalker, again and again missing the mark. "Missing the mark" is precisely the biblical figure for sin *(hamartia)*. The sinner is a fool and unrealist whose arrow repeatedly flies by the target, a person whose bad judgment frustrates both self and society.

Now, for the Bible and most traditional books of wisdom, the distinction between judging (asserting or denying) and deciding is not so crisp as the modern epistemologist might make it. Only long centuries of studying human reason, especially in the light of its spectacular successes in modern science, have brought the epistemological nuance that is available today. On the other hand, modern epistemologists sometimes miss an important truth that the Bible and older philosophies kept front and center. This is the mutual influence of judging and deciding, being and acting. When the Bible says that only the person who does the truth comes to the light (John 3:21), it practically defines the nature of moral or religious truth. When we are talking about a truth that can make or break human health, we must include the will as much as the intellect. In fact, we must focus on the heart, the central integrity of the person that lies beneath any distinction between intellect and will. When the heart is sound, the person acts in keeping with his or her judgments. When the heart is sound, the person's actions set up another round of good judgments, because they bring the person into working contact with reality as it is, in contrast to reality as the sinner tries to twist it for personal gain.

So the assertions or denials of good judgments are not ends in themselves. In concrete, actual life (in distinction from such truncations as merely academic study), people must deal with an imperative to decide and follow through. The truth (the reality I have found in my prejudgmental reflective survey) being such and such, what am I going to do about it? For example, the truth being that smoking ruins the lungs and injures other organs, what am I going to do about my habit of puffing two packs a day? The truth being that exercise prolongs life and enhances health, what am I going to do about my vegetation? The truth being that Janie's late nights and guilty looks suggest that her relation with Tommy is no longer platonic, what am I (her father) going to do about it? The truth being that I can't stand my colleague, what am I going to do about my need to vote on his promotion? Again and again, what we judge involves us in decisions about what we shall do. If the experience of insight (grasping what might be so) tends to require that we enter into the experience of verification (finding out what actually is so), the experience of judging what is or is not so tends to require that we enter into the experience of deciding what we are going to do, whether we are going to conform our actions with reality.

Those who do not conform their actions with reality, do not at least strive for a symmetry between their doing and their knowing, are hypocrites. They may raise smoke screens to obscure their inconsistencies, may rationalize their not following through, but in their hearts they will suffer the sadness of being hollow, the self-disgust of the sinner who knows he or she is missing the mark. You cannot miss the mark of personal integrity unknowingly, guiltlessly. The coincidence of being and doing, knowing and performing, is at the center of human selfhood. Not those who say "Lord, Lord" but those who do the Lord's will enter the kingdom. Not those who know and hold back but those who do the deeds of love enjoy good conscience, sleep the sleep of the just.

## Having an Open Soul

The difference between the hypocrite and the *Mensch,* the person who is really human, is that the one tolerates a gap between knowing and doing while the other strives tirelessly to close that gap, make knowing and doing run in tandem. The *Mensch* will not always succeed, of course. Not even the best of the saints perfectly fulfill their visions. But the *Mensch* will keep trying, always will want to be a man who keeps his word, a woman who acts according to her best lights. The hypocrite will be slow to confess inconsistencies, failures to perform, gaps between professing and enacting. The hypocrite will be quick to rationalize, shift the rules of the game, stonewall and doublespeak. The degeneration of public language in our time is chilling evidence that hypocrisy has now become close to standard practice. If stonewalling, doublespeaking, and outright lying have become normal coin, as the Watergate hearings and their successors suggest they have become in Washington, the national mind is close to accepting hypocrisy as commonplace. But people who can't say what they know, can't do what they know, or can't do what they say manifestly are alienated, warped, sinful. If they are the leaders, or even the movers and shakers of a nation, that nation is spiritually bereft.

"Things were ever thus," some of you may be saying, and your saying unfortunately seems true. For example, almost four thousand years ago an unknown Egyptian poet composed a dialogue with his soul in which he debated the pros and cons of suicide. Among the pros, the inducements to ending his life, bulked large the spiritual disease of his society:

> To whom can I speak today? One's fellows are evil; the friends of today do not love. To whom can I speak today? Faces have disappeared: Every man has a downcast face toward his fellow. To whom can I speak today? A man should arouse wrath by his evil character, but he stirs everyone to laughter, in spite of the wickedness of his sin. To whom can I speak today? There are no righteous; the land is left to those who do wrong. To whom can I speak today? The sin that afflicts the land, it has no end.[1]

However, the fact that hypocrisy and sin have pockmarked most human societies most of the time should not lead to our countenancing them. It perhaps should keep us from being shattered when we see them occurring, but it should not cause us to deny something more significant that we know in our bones or at the center of our souls. This is our call to a consistency between knowing and doing, our sureness that sin is irrational, self-violating, radically inhuman. As a somewhat trivial example, I remember riding with a person who at first was amused and then irritated by my expectation that other drivers would use their signals when turning.

"They just don't do that here," my passenger said. "It doesn't matter that it's the law or good driving, they just don't do it."

"Fine, they don't do it," I said. "I'll not presume that no signal means no turn. But I'll also not stop making signals myself, and not stop criticizing other drivers for not making them. It's one thing to recognize that irrationality is occurring and take that irrationality into account. It's another thing to start calling irrationality normality and bending one's behavior out of shape to accommodate to it."

The conversion, healing, and return to sanity that redeems a hypocrite and makes a *Mensch* is an opening of the midmost spirit. Confucius used to talk about the midmost spirit or midmost mind when he wanted to indicate the center that conviction has to reach if a person is to become genuinely ethical or human, not just someone who puts on a good act or shows a glossy veneer. In Christian terms, it is the midmost mind that is opened when the Spirit orients us to the divine Mystery, sparks the gap between our knowing and our doing, and gives us the courage to pledge that we will try to become whole. When the divine Mystery draws near and scatters our secular idols, our temptations to twist the truth, or to say one thing and do another, fade perceptibly. Almost always hypocrites ply their trade, work their self-twistings, for temporary advantages. Money and power are the most popular causes, the reasons that dominate the congressional hearings. But religious influence can also turn people hypocritical, as it apparently had turned the Pharisees whom Jesus pilloried.

If the Gospels portray Jesus' accusations accurately (in some passages the Gospels, especially Matthew, are suspect of partisan bias—sniping at early Christianity's most formidable Jewish enemies), the Pharisees who got the rough side of Jesus' tongue cared less for the glory of God or the comfort of their people than for their own status and influence. They gloried in the niceties, the subtleties, the virtuosities of the Law rather than in the heart of the religious matter: mercy, compassion, love. They prayed to list their supposed virtues, rather than to petition God to heal their deep sin. People with open souls do not pray or live that way, "pharisaically." People with open souls count themselves sinners, profitless servants, people doing far too little for their neighbors. The religious leaders whom Jesus castigated were hypocrites because they had no loving, real God. Many of our political and religious leaders ring hollow, command no respect, because their souls are not open to the divine Mystery. That a solid percentage of each citizenry always does stay open to the divine Mystery shows the great mercies of Christ's grace.

# 6.

# THE DISCERNMENT OF SPIRITS

*Ordinary Stirrings of God's Spirit*

Let the midmost spirit or mind be open, and the Spirit of God will have no trouble working a person's steady progress. This may be nothing spectacular, but in time it can produce a person wise as a serpent yet innocent as a dove. The Spirit is a teacher of realism, a pedagogue concerned that pupils mature and grow balanced. So the lessons that take the pupil up in exaltation, revealing the outlines of what faith says we may hope, have counterbalances in lessons of humility, where the pupil learns that all flesh is grass. The realistic, balanced assessment is that we strange creatures are both a little less than the angels and but dust and ashes. When the dust and ashes threaten to snuff out our hopes, the Spirit quickens us, brooding over our bent world with warm breast and ah! bright wings. When our angelic reason and will threaten to turn Promethean, Faustian, the Spirit lets us taste how little we are or can do on our own. Kierkegaard perceived the irony of all this when, surfeited with the pretenses of Hegel's System, he observed how comic it was that the Great Mind in whom the World Spirit was vouchsafing its revelations had to turn aside like an ordinary mortal to sneeze.

I propose, therefore, that we consider our ordinary lessons in realism to be stirrings of the Holy Spirit. Whatever teaches us our proper place in the divine scheme of things, intimates how we should regard ourselves, is fitting us to the mind of Christ, bringing us to the measure God has in mind for us, and so is attributable to the Spirit. The lessons in angelic potential, counterbalanced by the lessons in dust and ashes, are but one specimen of the Spirit's pedagogy. The Lutheran tag *simul justus et peccator* points to many another. We are at one and the same time both people whom God has justified and people who are sinners.

Our justification is as objective as the life, death, resurrection, and work of Jesus Christ. We cannot abandon our confession of this justification without losing our grip on faith, becoming either faithless or heretical. Moreover, we cannot confess our justification with our lips and not look for it, seek its experiential meaning or operation, in our daily lives. To do that would be to introduce the sort of schism or gap that in the last chapter we laid at the door of hypocrites. No, to say that we are justified is to say that at least now and then our souls do seem to be open, the Spirit does seem to list, and we do seem to be carried out to the oceanic Mystery of our loving God. For all its chaos, disorder, and raging evils, the world does have still points, grace notes, moments and creatures of breathtaking beauty. These could not be ours, as we undeniably know them to be, were we not somehow right with God, the Father of Lights from whom all good gifts descend.

On the other hand, at the very same time, we remain sinners, people who owe their justification to another, people who have not rooted out their rebellion against God. Augustine spoke of sin as love of self unto contempt of God. In his view it was a perversion of right order, an absurd or complete lack of reason, caused by self-idolization. The church catholic has taught that none of us escapes this sort of tainted self-love. Only Jesus (and, for branches of the church, Mary) was born like us in all things save sin. Only Jesus loved without taint, in complete reason and confession of God. The rest of us, for all our justification and right to the title "saints," have willing spirits but weak flesh, do not do some goods we should do and do do some evils we should not do.

The Spirit teaches us lessons in justification and sinfulness with an increasingly fine hand. If in the beginning the lessons seem stark, proportioned to our grossness and inexperience, by the maturity of a long life of faith the lessons are quite subtle, both dazzling and humbling us with the variety of graces and sins they detail. So the saints become great guardians of their senses, their imaginations, their idle thoughts. So the moralists, both Christian and Buddhist, can distinguish layer upon layer of motivation, intention, purity or cloudedness of spirit. The main tension remains what it was at the beginning. We continue to be both justified and sinners. But the richness of each side of this polarity, and the mystery of the two sides' fusion, admits of limitless nuance. Without any mystical raptures or seizures, the Spirit can make ordinary days, weeks, months, and years matter of increasing illumination. If we will but attend, abide, try to open ourselves, we can learn at least a little of the wisdom that the biblical sages so touted, receive at least a little of the gracious largess that the Lady Chokhmah (Wisdom) symbolized for Jesus' people.

We best begin the discernment of spirits, then, with strong faith that God can teach us the things for our peace through quite ordinary experiences. We need not go to extraordinary places, undertake extraordinary disciplines, leave family or business life to become good students of the Spirit. We need only practice reflection, consecrate some quiet, open our hearts regularly, and pray. If we worry the Lord, like the widow with the unjust judge, or the friend needing bread, we can find justification and nourishment. Indeed, if we but open the door, we find that Christ has long been knocking.

## *Implications of Grace*

If we are willing to open to Christ's knocking, let the Spirit do the love-work the Spirit wishes, we may begin to discern how the unfolding of our lives is a family affair. Indeed, we may begin to sense, at least dimly, that the processes of natural evolution and human history belong to us, in miniature, somewhat the way that they belong to God. For the midmost implication of grace is that God so takes our part, sends out waves of favor toward us, that our part becomes God's own cause, our beings become sharers of the divine nature. A connaturality arises between us and God, as grace penetrates our beings, such that God sees us in the lines of Christ, thinks of us as members of Christ. What Israel conceived as a covenant between the people and their God has become, as Jeremiah foresaw, a new, interiorized compact, written by the Spirit in our hearts. When that new, interior law rules our consciousnesses, all the things of God are ours, because we are Christ's and Christ is God's. The communion that grows from any love, the commonweal and common cause, sends forth tendrils of an organism that one day would clearly reveal our engagement in the ongoing creation of the world. The destiny it suggests we bear even now is cocreation, conspiracy, collaboration in God's *mysterion* (plan), as Paul called it, which from the foundations of the world has been guiding the unfolding of the universe.

This is heady stuff, well suggested by scripture but virtually impossible to pin down. Like all ultimate or religious language, it is more poetic than scientific, more evocative or allusive than literal or denotative. Trying to suggest something of their mind-boggling experiences of Jesus and the Spirit, the Christians who forged the New Testament threw out bits of imagery, pieces of suggestion from the Hebrew Bible, thoughts and hopes that came from their knowing Jesus in the breaking of bread. The central themes around which these poetic expressions of their deepest experiences circled included the notion of sharing in the very life of Father, Son, and Spirit, and the notion that this sharing was missionary: something given them for the sake of the whole world. The Christian good news, as the first generation of its preachers clarified it, was not simply an infra-Jewish thing. Especially for Paul and John, Jesus' messiahship had roots in the very structure of the universe. As the Logos, the divine Word, Jesus was the enfleshment of the blueprint from which creation, both natural and human, was drawn.

The Logos is the image (icon) of the fathomless divine source, so it is sensible to picture all things in "creation" (a finite, partial expression of and sharing in the divine infinity) as having come into being through him. Moreover, it makes sense to speak of the Incarnation as larger or more comprehensive than creation, and to speak of creation as Christocentric. Those who do not want to accept the literal incarnation of the Logos (and so the traditional "high Christology" of the classical councils of Nicaea and Chalcedon) will place different emphases,[1] but these seem to me the most faith filled.

Now, the point to this excursus into Christology is not to shift from a book on Christian conscience to a book on speculative theology but to situate the grace that should dominate and form a Christian conscience. Christian grace is the grace of Christ, the favor and divine life that God has poured forth in and through Jesus of Nazareth. When Jesus associated his followers with himself as branches to vine, he implied that the Christian community would participate in the relations he bears the Father and the Spirit. Both the "immanent" relations (those occurring "within" the life of the Trinity, without reference to creation) and the "economic" relations (those occurring in the orders of salvation and creation in time) become ours, in a derivative or adoptive sense. The structure of our divine lives (our sharing in the divine nature) is not just Trinitarian but Christocentric (or Logocentric). We stand receptive toward the Father, identified with the

Son, "spirative" (breathing) of the Spirit with the Father and Son. (Eastern Christians, who conceive the spiration of the Spirit as solely the work of the Father, would shift the imagery somewhat.) Thus the Father plays a special symbolic role in our sense of the origin, the uncaused causality, the fathomless source of everything. The Son plays a special symbolic role in our self-conception, and also in our sense of the Reason or Order according to which creation and salvation occur. The Spirit plays a special symbolic role in our sense of the love by which all things are animated, vivified, made whole and beautiful.

Brooded over, ruminated, tasted in the way that wisdom-ventures do ("wisdom"—*sapientia*—is etymologically cognate to "taste"—*sapor*), these images shed some light, give some flavor, to the experiences that play in the depths of our spirits, where the Spirit teaches, consoles, prays in our heart-to-heart intercourse with God. The imagery is too rich, too unconstrainable, for us ever to set it in tidy channels, but again and again it encourages us to believe that we have been inserted into the innermost design of God's dynamic creation. Thus Teilhard de Chardin finally came to speak of "Christogenesis": the becoming of the Whole Christ, Head and Members, who is the Alpha and Omega of physical evolution (Biogenesis, Noogenesis). The imagery also anoints our flesh, ratifies our humanity and history, for it all waves forth from an incarnate divine Reason, a Logos that took flesh, became what we are, made time the spouse of eternity.

## *Beginners and the Mature*

While all Christians share in a grace that has these Trinitarian and christological overtones, the themes that the Spirit seems apt to emphasize vary with the time and state of one's sharing. I say "seems apt to emphasize" because there is no constraining the Spirit, no charting the Spirit's ways in textbook fashion. At one point in the film of the *Long Search* series that deals with Catholicism, the narrator is discussing prayer with a Spanish Benedictine monk. The monk says flatly that the Holy Spirit is the only master of prayer. It is what the Spirit prompts, inspires, demands that becomes the rule or protocol of our prayer, not what the books say the Spirit will prompt. Not only can God raise up children of Abraham from inert stones, God can take people from zero to sixty in the twinkling of an eye, the mere fall from a horse, if that be God's desire. What is impossible with human beings is quite possible with God. If we had sufficient faith, God might uproot our mountains of sinfulness and cast them into the sea.

With this said, however, it remains that usually it is useful to acquaint oneself with what the masters have written on prayer and the discernment of spirits. I say this not merely because I sympathize with people who have gone to the trouble of setting their thoughts down on paper. I say it also because it is manifestly true: To read John of the Cross, or John Wesley, or Simeon the New Theologian is to put oneself in dialogue with the profound and living tradition of Christian faith. Just as the Spirit seems frequently to take over a passage of scripture, bringing its words to shining life, warming our hearts with the ancient, well-polished phrases, so the Spirit seems inclined to impregnate Christian spiritual classics. Thus the sayings of the desert fathers can become eloquent on Park Avenue. The *Imitation of Christ* can put new music in Nashville. Contrary to what superficial prediction might suggest, the Spirit can cross centuries and continents to drive home the lesson that human beings share a radical equality before God. All of us are creatures, utterly dependent on God for our barest being. All of us are sinners, cleansed only to the extent that we have been washed by the blood of the Lamb. Sharing one Lord, one faith, one baptism, we should not be surprised that we share many religious insights, religious needs, religious experiences in prayer. The pioneers of our faith who hacked their way through the forest, the cloud of witnesses who preceded us in testing, can be immensely helpful. Listening to the chorus of the whole 144,000 (Rev. 7:4), we can slowly grow attuned to the melody that fills God's highest heaven: Worthy is the Lamb that was slain to receive all honor and glory and power and riches.

Frequently the Spirit shocks people into beginning to contend with these things by revealing the brevity of life, the closeness of death, the repulsiveness of sin. A beginner is someone whose hold on the realism of faith, the constant need to magnify God and give thanks for God's bounteous gifts, is weak. A mature believer is someone who has chewed on these fundamentals long enough to have gotten them into her marrow. A beginner needs consolations of the Spirit strong enough to make her glad to be out of the realm of darkness, away from the world that opposes God. So beginning faith frequently is ecstatic, emotional, filled with sweetness and light. If it paints the horrors of sin and hell in vivid colors, so does it paint the delights of grace and heaven. This painting is not wrong, but it is somewhat provisional.

The realities of faith do not exist for our warning or delectation. We are not the center in any mature religious vision, any adequate religious depiction. The pains of sin are the inevitable consequences of lovelessness, just as the delights of grace are the inevitable consequences of God's love. Neither are ends in themselves, things that the mature aim directly to avoid or gain. The mature aim to avoid the idolatry and amnesia that keep us from making the living, mysterious God our wholehearted treasure, not as a riches that would enhance our spiritual bank account but as the objective love that moves the stars, the objective beauty by which the world stands. A mature praise of God is nothing concocted, whipped up, dependent on anything as fragile as emotional euphoria. The praise of God that the 144,000 hymn is the simple, straightforward truth-telling of eyes that see, ears that hear, hearts that love and so understand.

To move us toward this straightforward praise of God, this *eucharistia* that would be the depth of each waking moment rather than just an emotional peak of Sunday morning, the Spirit often produces dark nights or clouds of unknowing. "Dark nights," which recall the imagery of John of the Cross, purify first the senses and then the ground of the spirit, to teach us that God is as real as the air and the trees, the flesh on our arms and the thoughts in our heads. To become this realistic, we have to be stripped of our instinctive sensationalism, ego-centricity, and unwillingness to move beyond what we know. "Clouds of unknowing," which recall the central imagery of the medieval classic *The Cloud of Unknowing,* are overshadowings of our imagination and reason by the divine Mystery. Become immediate, drawn near to confront us or make overtures to our spirits directly, God seems opaque, thick, no thing we can handle. In either image, the point is the same: The mature are those on a path to direct experience of God, naked encounter, entry into the darkness necessary for us who cannot bear God's blinding light.

## True and False Leadings

True leadings, genuine inspirations of the Holy Spirit, produce the classical fruit that Paul described in Galatians 5: "But the fruit of the Spirit is love, joy, peace, patience, kindness, goodness, faithfulness, gentleness, self-control" (Gal. 5:22–23). False leadings produce pride, sensuality, aversion from God, and the other marks of what Paul called "flesh." When Jesus counseled us to look to people's fruits (rather than their words), he anticipated Paul's pragmatism. The crux of Christian discernment is the overall effect that a particular way, discipline, belief, or practice is having. If, overall, it is building up the individual's faith and helping the community, it likely is a good way. If it is tending to roil the individual's spirit or disturb the community's peace, it likely is a bad way.

Sometimes we have to try a way for a while, give it time to show what fruits it will grow. The esteemed Rabbi Gamaliel was thinking in this vein when he advised the leaders of the Jewish council to leave Peter and the other early Christian preachers alone: "I tell you, keep away from these men and let them alone; for if this plan or this undertaking is of men, it will fail; but if it is of God, you will not be able to overthrow them. You might even be found opposing God!" (Acts 5:38–39). A good tree cannot produce bad fruit, and a bad tree cannot (consistently, reliably) produce good fruit. We can know true and false leadings by their fruits.

Still, it may be helpful to specify how good fruits usually glisten and taste. First, there is the matter of balance and stability. The Spirit of God is not capricious, sensational, in for only the short haul. Those who insist on euphoria, quick fixes, impressive numbers, and the like don't know the ways of the Spirit. It is characteristic of the Spirit to remind those who are flying high that they can easily crash, those who are beaten down that in patience they can possess their souls. Without fearing or despising high emotion, the Spirit seems on the whole to prefer a quiet warmth, a sober peace. Without being unwilling to teach us through success, the Spirit seems on the whole to imprint the deepest lessons through failure. This is not cruelty or perverseness. It is no contradiction of the notion that the love of God interweaves with a healthy self-love. It is simply how things tend to go with us sinners, us resistant, intractable lumps of clay.

For the Spirit to mold us into vessels at all fit, much misconception and recalcitrance have to break down. We don't willingly leave the path of easy consolations, fancy visions, sweet emotions. The cross of Christ is as far from our liking as it was from Peter and the other apostles, who fled from it like the plague. At the least, the Spirit has to teach us the distance between God's ways and our human own. As the heavens are above the earth, so are God's ways higher, more inscrutable, stranger than we initially imagine. At the most, the Spirit must fit some of us to the corpus of Christ extended on the cross. If they have treated the Master thus, so shall they treat some of the disciples. And so they do—in the Soviet Union, Latin America, and so many other spots of the world that the heart grows woeful.

One may say, then, that a true leading of the Spirit faces up to Christ's cross, while a false leading either shuns the cross or embraces it foolishly. The shunning is more frequent. From time immemorial, the false prophets and the preachers of cheap grace have described Christianity without the cross, as a thing of pink Cadillacs or sales bonuses. In our country the collusion of this denatured Christianity with capitalistic greed is a major scandal. All that Jesus said about bewaring wolves in sheeps' clothing rings relevant today. One can no more serve God and Mammon now than one could when Jesus preached.

Indeed, one of the most challenging lessons being read out to the whole church today comes from the liberation theologians, who make painfully clear God's preference for the poor, the suffering, the oppressed. If one looks today for the population of the Beatitudes, today's equivalent of Jesus' *anawim* (poor of Yahweh), it is not the country clubs or ecclesiastical mansions that seem most promising. The poor of Yahweh are those whose material and spiritual circumstances make them hungry for God, aware of their need, open to the nearly incredible good news of the Kingdom. The gospel has always been "social" in this sense. It is no innovation at all to say that God is on the side of the outcast. From the time of Mary's "Magnificat" Christianity has declared God's predilection for the poor and lowly: "He has scattered the proud in the imagination of their hearts, he has put down the mighty from their thrones, and exalted those of low degree; he has filled the hungry with good things, and the rich he has sent empty away" (Luke 1:51–53).

False leadings would so spiritualize this good news that it no longer bore on people's real sufferings. Like the docetic Christ, the early heretics' Messiah who only appeared to be fully human, false leadings don't want to engage actual hunger, pain, injustice, or doubt. They would eviscerate Christianity of its living center: a Word who became flesh, knew our life from within, really lived, really died, really rose. True leadings would make faith as concrete as bread, wine, water, a kiss of peace. True leadings would make our superfluities over to those who lack necessities, make us peacemakers, people pure in heart, people willing to suffer for righteousness' sake.

## Consolation without Previous Cause

In Saint Ignatius Loyola's famous handbook, *The Spiritual Exercises,* two sets of rules (for beginners and for the mature) differentiate the motions (experiences) of the soul into those attributable to the good Spirit and those attributable to "the enemy of our human nature." In making his analysis Loyola places great importance on the difference between *consolation* and *desolation.* The former, which is a summary term for all the things that build up faith, hope, and love, is the work of the good Spirit. All who are making a solid effort to progress in Christian faith can be sure that God is their encourager, helper, Paraclete. The latter, which is a summary term for all the things that militate against faith and discourage religious effort, is the doing of the enemy of our human nature.

However, it takes some wisdom to know, in more advanced cases, what actually is building up faith, hope, and love and what actually is militating against them. Satan may appear as an angel of light, lifting people up in false exaltation. Only by careful attention to the fruits of a consolation will its truth or falsity come clear. If the consoling emotions slowly pass over into more sensual, prideful, faithless states of spirit, they will reveal the tail of the serpent. On the other hand, dryness of soul, testing of faith, purification in dark nights of the senses or the spirit may prove to be the work of God. If the person, even when feeling abandoned, finds the strength to call upon God, try to persevere in generous loving, place his sufferings in God's hands, every likelihood is that one day a much stronger consolation will break through, perhaps to take him into unitive living: full communion with God, the ability to find the divine presence in all things.

When Loyola wants to describe the least ambiguous case of consolation, the surest sign of God's work in the human soul, he speaks of "consolation without previous cause." ("It is characteristic only of God to give consolation to the soul without previous cause.")[2] The reason Ignatius gives for this is that (only) the Creator has the property of entering, leaving, and making movements in the soul, drawing everything into love of the Creator's divine majesty. The Creator may do this without any previous sensation or awareness of another object—immediately, directly, in utter freedom. This may be a rather rare occurrence (all that we said in defense of the Spirit's ordinary stirrings, which use our normal sensations, emotions, thoughts, and volitions, suggests that it is), but it shows at least one indisputable time when God is at work within us. Let consolation sweep in without any preparation, anticipation, attributable cause, and we may suspect that God has moved our soul directly. The effect is so out of proportion to the other possible causes that the other possible causes do not suffice. Nothing in what we had been thinking, doing, eating, planning, gave any hint that we would soon be swept into a total, devouring love of the divine majesty. The only explanation is the Spirit's having chosen to move that way, love us that gratuitously, so surprise us with joy.

Many people report moments such as this, and although not all of them stand up to careful scrutiny, enough do stand up to make it plain that God is quite incalculable, never agrees to stay peaceably in our back pockets. When C. S. Lewis speaks of being "surprised by joy," he points in the direction of Loyola's consolation without previous cause. The pure joy that came to him was utterly unexpected, utterly gracious. Ever after it sang at the base of his spirit like a quiet, sustaining plainchant. The biologist Lewis Thomas describes a moment of analogous grace that came to him in the Tucson Zoo.[3] He had been watching some otters and beavers larking in the water when suddenly their splendor took him out of himself and painted the world aglow. This is only an analogue, because one can point to predisposing experiences and because his being swept away in love of the divine majesty was only implicit. But it shows that many people do have powerful experiences that a deterministic psychology could never expect, and that some of these experiences shape them for good for the rest of their lives. (Thus, even if they are disputable in their occurring, their good fruits argue that such experiences come from the God who has left witness everywhere.)

Loyola's caution regarding peak consolations is that one must distinguish carefully between the actual time of the consolation's occurrence, which tends to be dominated by the pure presence of God and love of the divine majesty, and the times that succeed the occurrence, when human reasoning usually comes into play. Not every deduction from the pure experience will be warranted. The thoughts that we have after the fact do not share the high authority of the unmediated experience itself. Were we to let thoughts of pride and self-satisfaction overwhelm us, the enemy of our human nature might destroy much of the good the Creator had done us.

Still, consolations without previous cause, or any times when things fall into place and God's love seems obvious, tend to linger in the memories of the devout as touchstones, trailblazings, templates on which they later rely. Those were times when we knew what we were made for. Our mind was clear, our heart had biblical measure, pressed down and overflowing. Therefore those are times that can interpret our later confusions, doubts, ambiguities. Until God clearly foreswears such times, clearly shows them to have been illusory, they should function for us as the Exodus functioned for Israel: as revelatory paradigms, key moments that illumine all our subsequent history.

$$7.$$

# DIALOGUE WITH GOD

## *From Examination to Prayer*

When we examine our consciences regularly, using the quiet of early morning and late night to try to discern what the Spirit of God has been moving us to think and feel, we make practical our faith in divine providence. That faith says that God runs the world, has a plan, lets not a hair of our heads be ruffled without God's knowledge. If so, the inner experiences we have, our senses of consolation and desolation, must be under God's guidance. God is not responsible for them in a way that would take away our freedom, but God is the potter molding them into the substance of our lives, the intimate partner to a covenant we have committed ourselves to let unfold through time. Since everything in our lives has time's Mystery as its context or backdrop, everything in our lives is referable to God. If we believe God's word, everything in our lives suggests God's love and care for us, God's interest in us. When the psalmist asked God to deal with him as the apple of His eye, the psalmist reflected a deep faith in God's providence. When Jesus told the disciples to consider the lilies of the field, he bade them be hopeful that God would carry them through.

The step from examining our consciences (to see how the processes of providence have been faring) to praying to God can be small and easy. Let the thoughts, problems, hopes, or affections we have been experiencing but reach out to the Mystery of their origin, context, depth, or term, and we find ourselves "at" God. Let our hearts but address this God, but praise or petition God, and we are in the midst of the dialogue so crucial to Christian religion, the prayerful exchanges that actualize the life of grace. The life of grace, we have repeatedly seen, is our sharing in the very divine nature. For this to be more than an empty symbol, it must become the main interpretational framework of our nights and days. Below what honors we have won in the community, what we have racked up on the stock market, how we are progressing in our profession, even how we are doing with our spouse and children lies the most basic interpretational reference point: our dealings with our Creator. Since our Creator has chosen to make these dealings (whether they be explicit or merely implicit) a family affair, something situated midst the eternal exchanges of Father, Son, and Spirit, we ought to do our best to use a familial "hermeneutic" (interpretational key).

If we do use a familial hermeneutic, we almost automatically begin addressing God prayerfully. Jesus' example in this regard is overwhelmingly clear. What we call the "Lord's Prayer" is but the formalization of the steady, regular, daily recourse that Jesus had to his Father. For Jesus the will of his Abba ("Daddy") was meat and drink, the bone and marrow of his life. He and the Father were one, in the psychology of his human motivation as well as the ontology of his eternal relation to his source. Jesus would have defined himself (had anyone ever asked him such a question) wholly in terms of his Father. He had come to do the Father's will, preach the Father's kingdom, make manifest the Father's love. The mutual love of his disciples was crucial because it would be the evidence of the Father's love for the world. The Father had given the only begotten Son to manifest this love and make the world right. As Paul saw, since the Father has given us this best of all possible gifts, how can he fail to give us everything else that he has to give?

Indeed, when Paul uses the word *God (ho theos)* he means the Father of Jesus Christ. When he makes reference to the mystery of God's plan, he implies the Trinitarian relations, the family business into which God's saving grace has invited all human beings. So Paul's transition from an examination of conscience or a theological speculation to prayer is quick and easy. He need only slightly personalize the reflection, slightly sharpen its existential point, and it becomes an exclamation of praise for God's surpassing bounty, a petition for God's help against our recalcitrant sin.

Further, one suspects that Paul's prayers, like those of Jesus, often settled into a quiet, wordless, simple being-with God, the Father, Son, and Spirit. When Jesus withdrew into solitude to pray and recuperate, he was giving himself the opportunity to turn his mind and heart to the Mystery full-time, undistractedly. Then the name of the Father who was in heaven, the realm of divine perfection, might be properly hallowed. Then the impetus for the kingdom to come could be fully intense. The same with the other phrases of the Lord's Prayer. One suspects that they are but verbalizations of dispositions that played in Jesus' being constantly, with sighs too deep for words.

And so, in much humbler scope, can it be for us, if we will but turn our faces toward God. Everything that we hope, everything that we need, everything for which we ought to give thanks has a reference to the divine Mystery. What we find when we scrape the shingles of our spirits, do the housekeeping of the examination of conscience, is not significant in itself. Its significance comes from the positive or negative pressure it exerts on the overall drift of our lives, the overall plan of God into which we have been inserted. Any increase of good, in either the overall drift of our lives or the overall plan of God, comes from God. Quickly, therefore, the examination may become an opening of our hands and spirits to God.

## More Implications of Grace

Existentializing the examination of conscience, putting a personal accent on the things we have been experiencing and focusing our review of them toward the divine Mystery, takes us into the Trinitarian processions. The roots of conscience are the "speaking" by which the Father generates the Word and the "breathing" by which the Spirit proceeds from the Father and the Son. At the same time, making the examination of conscience prayerful means situating it in the processes of salvation and redemption. The same grace that elevates us into the personal life of the Godhead is at work to win us back from sin, make us whole and clean. This saving or healing dimension of grace unveils further implications that any adequate view of Christian conscience has to factor.

Through the long history of its ponderings of revelation, Christian tradition has gravitated toward a centrist position on most complicated problems. Concerning the problem of the relation between nature and grace, for example, the mainstream of the tradition has proposed complementarity or harmony rather than a radical discontinuity. Something in nature (what the Scholastics called an "obediential potency") reaches out for grace, providing God the "opening" needed to pour in the divine love life. The outreach of our minds, which beg a beatific vision, and the outreach of our hearts, which ask for an unlimited love, are both somewhat infinite. Even though we must reason and love piecemeal, unlike the total and instantaneous understanding and love of pure spirits, we cannot conceive of anything but God as satisfying our minds or hearts. Indeed, this is a major reason that we have a significant freedom. Since nothing finite can compel our minds or hearts, nothing finite forces us to give ourselves to it. Were we to see God directly, encounter the infinite divine beauty and goodness unveiled, we would not be free to turn away. (In choosing an incarnate form, therefore, God has found a way to leave our love free.)

The symmetry between human nature and divine grace, however, is not such that nature ever has a right to God's inmost personal life. This would be true even if human nature were not marred by sin, but it is doubly true of fallen humanity. The coming of the Spirit therefore is the healing as well as the perfecting of human nature. The Spirit washes what is dirtied, cures what is sickened, makes lucid what is opaque. To a nature created good but twisted by sin, the Spirit offers a wondrous homecoming. The ways of God, initially so foreign, slowly become ways we see should be native. Reason and love, which we find so hard to make sovereign, gradually become obvious, at least as ideals. And then the irrationality of such massive evils as human wars and preparations for wars stands out as truly satanic. It is not "natural" for human beings to treat one another worse than wolves. It is the success of Loyola's "enemy of our human nature."

This is all standard enough stuff, the normal meditational material one can derive from the traditional treatises on redemptive grace. It becomes personally relevant when we let it reshape our practical view of the human nature we meet at work and in the kitchen. What about my colleagues, whom so much in my culture inclines me to consider heartless competitors? Is it possible that I and they have wandered into a crazy dance that none of us ever wanted? Could it be that we have it in us to blow the whistle, stop the music, and reset all the measures toward peace and cooperation? The extraordinary perceptions of the few fully human beings that history has produced, the exceptional saints and people of wisdom, suggest that the lion could lie down with the lamb were either to be shocked into full consciousness. A Francis of Assisi or Mohandas Gandhi shows us what human nature could be, were we to drop the defense mechanisms that keep us from dealing with other creatures openly, trustingly, encouragingly. Lucas Grollenberg's winning little portrait of Jesus[1] makes the case that Jesus was extraordinarily human precisely because he did not need to protect himself the way the rest of us feel that we must. He could float in utter repose on the fathomless being of his Father and so had to fear no human being, reject no human being as threatening.

Thomas à Kempis, author of *The Imitation of Christ,* moaned that whenever he went out into society he came back less a man. When I come back from social excursions I marvel at how little humanity I have either seen or contributed. The talk has been trivial, the interaction guarded, the whole dispersion of time disappointing. Once again we have connived, the others and I, to waste time, slip by one another, confirm one another's suspicion that most people are boring, not worth much bother. Surely this so frequent experience of original sin, which much worse examples could trump, shows us major implications that the Spirit would give to Christian grace, major therapies. Indeed, when we beg the Spirit's regenerative energies in prayer, ask the Spirit to reform our consciences into something worthy of our divine calling, we petition a complete transformation of society, the entire "new creation" of which Paul spoke. From cocktail parties and board-room meetings to new economic, political, cultural, and ecclesiastical systems, the grace of the Spirit would make our time and space sacramental: something to bring out the image of God we presently smudge, the love of God we presently stifle. The further implications of grace are radical indeed, as the Baptist promised: "He will baptize you with the Holy Spirit and with fire. His winnowing fork is in his hand, and he will cleanse his threshing floor and gather his wheat into the granary, but the chaff he will burn with unquenchable fire" (Matt. 3:11–12).

## Jesus as Companion

The Jesus who will bring about this radical challenge to human beings, confronting them with a *kairos* or time of judgment, is the Jesus to whom the *Imitation of Christ,* Loyola's *Spiritual Exercises,* and many other classics of Christian prayer would have us pray. For while the masters regularly speak of God's overshadow-ing of our minds in prayer, how meditation on concepts must give way to contemplation of God's living mystery, they also insist that Jesus himself is a prime object of contemplation. The Eastern Orthodox tradition, which has produced such a splendid iconography, has made this long-held Christian conviction the basis of its liturgical art. In their solemn portraits of Jesus, Mary, and the saints, Orthodox artists have represented their bedrock faith in the Incarnation. God has so taken flesh, so pitched his tent in our midst, that everything material bears a presence of God, above all everything that Jesus has touched. Following Athanasius' dictum that "what was not assumed was not saved," the Eastern theologians have taught that everything human was assumed, the Incarnation took God as deeply into humanity as anyone could go. In fact, the person of the Word, the divine Son, was the bearer of the act of existence of Jesus of Nazareth. There were not two persons, two bearers of existence (divine and human), but only one. The two natures of the Word incarnate are mysteriously united in the one person. That is the faith that Athanasius championed at Nicaea and Cyril of Alexandria championed at Chalcedon. That is the faith that fifteen centuries have called "orthodox."

The resurrected Christ, seated at the right hand of the Father, now reigns in heavenly glory. Drawing on this doctrinal truth, the icon masters have portrayed Jesus as fraught with regal authority.[2] Many of their portraits seem to invite a petitionary mood, the state of mind that a subject would feel when having an audience with a sovereign. Perhaps the fusing of church and state in Eastern Christendom contributed to this mood, which found doctrinal expression in the notion that Christ is the Pantocrator, the Ruler of All. All powers, earthly and heavenly, come under his sway. No Caesar or Satan is the slightest match for him. Fittingly, therefore, his liturgy is like the ceremonial of a Byzantine court. Fittingly the incense rises, the tapers blaze, the holy doors close to shield the most sacred actions from unconsecrated eyes. We Westerners, who have largely lost our sense of solemn ritual, for whom the Super Bowl is high drama, can recapture a bit of what the Eastern centuries have celebrated by betaking ourselves to a Byzantine liturgy. As the chants unfold and the heavenly choirs are invoked, one senses how the East has felt the Spirit to pervade all creation, the Logos to be the inmost intelligibility of everything that exists. The church on earth is but a pale reflection of its heavenly model. The "Holy God, Holy Mighty, Holy Immortal" whom we petition for mercy is much more real than the terrestrial powers that fill the newspapers.

The Western approach to Jesus, as evidenced by Western art, is to lay greater stress on his humanity, in the sense of his nearness to us ordinary mortals. Be it nativity scenes or crucifixions, the Western masters have shown us a lovable baby, a victim broken for our sins, a holy man who loved us so deeply that he was willing to bear all our iniquities. Individual Christians, of course, have the freedom to use whatever imagery, Eastern or Western, they find most moving. Some people may find the Eastern tone of sovereignty powerful, intriguing, or refreshing. More Westerners are likely to find the Christ of humbler garb and more suffering mien deeply moving. Stripped of the sentimentality that often has corrupted it, the Western depiction of Christ crucified has managed to retain Paul's notion—that this is the prime stumbling block to Jewish faith and the prime foolishness to Gentile sensibility—without losing the Johannine sense that all of Christ's sufferings were borne out of love for us human beings, and that his being raised up on the cross was the definitive victory of love over hate.

Taking the Gospels as their prime meditational materials, millions of simple Christians have solved the practical problem of praying to God by engaging with the Christ who preached to the crowds, healed the sick, was transfigured before the disciples, walked the way of the cross, and confronted Mary in the garden, telling her to proclaim the resurrection to the rest of the disciples. This Jesus could be for such meditators what he had been for the twelve: Master, Rabbi, Lord. At moments of special intimacy he could be what he had been for John, the beloved disciple: the one on whose breast one might rest.

Whatever the best contemporary equivalent of these traditional associations, their core instinct remains not only valid but highly commendable. If we can identify with Jesus as the companion of our earthly time, the Master who knows what we endure because he endured it first, "God" may become much less distant, the Incarnation (which gives Christianity its distinctiveness among the world religions) may become much more formative of our faith. Jesus knew fatigue, discouragement, hunger, thirst, physical and emotional pain. As well, he knew joy, celebration, the conquest of temptation in the desert, the peace of commending his whole spirit into his Father's hands. So it is possible to go to him in labor, heavy burdened, and find rest. It is possible to take to him a great thirst and find living water. "Taste and see the goodness of the Lord," the psalmist and saints counsel. He remains the one Bread of Life.

## *Sharing Good and Bad*

Either with Jesus as the companion of its time, or through less imaginative prayer dealings with the Spirit, the maturing Christian conscience tends to develop the disposition that life-time is a basic stuff to be shared with God as thoroughly as possible. The biblical inclinations to this disposition include the self-revelation that God gives to Moses in Exodus 3, the intuition that Hosea has of God's marriage to Israel, the Pauline stress on Christ living in us, and the Johannine notion of abiding in Jesus and the Spirit. No doubt one could find other inclinations or stimuli in other biblical books, but these should suffice for our purposes.

When Moses receives God's name, it is, to say the least, elusive. "I am who I am" or "I am as I shall be with you" implies that we only learn who God is performatively, interactively, through the experience of sojourning with God through time. God is what we shall experience God to be, as God was for our ancestors what their time showed God to be. Their time is instructive for our time: Moses' experiences at the burning bush, on Mount Sinai, and in the Exodus have become central paradigms of biblical faith. But God is living, not encapsuled in texts, so each day brings new refinements to God's name, the sense we have of what God's creative mystery is working to accomplish.

Reflecting on the bond between the Mosaic God and the people of Israel, Hosea was saddened by the infidelities of the people, their failure to uphold their side of the covenant. This was so parallel to the painful state of his own marriage that he likened the infidelities of Israel to the infidelities of his wife Gomer. The likening brought an astounding possibility: perhaps God was as heartsore over Israel as Hosea was over Gomer. For he found that despite all his anger, hurt, and frustration he remained in love with Gomer, could not bear the thought of casting her out. And then, as is often the case with the analogical probings we make into the meaning of God's name, the nature of God's being, the similitude turned over. Clearly God had been much more long-suffering toward Israel than Hosea had been toward Gomer. Clearly God's steadfast, unconditional love was a challenge to him to try to muster a like generosity. If God was wholly committed, in for the longest of hauls, Hosea should try to be the same. If God wanted to share all of Israel's times, good and bad, he should want to marry himself to all of Gomer's times, moods, virtues, and failings.

The Pauline notion that the life of Christ in us is the deepest or most important thing about us leads to the same sort of "marital" dispositions. If we live, now not ourselves, but Christ lives in us, then to live is indeed Christ and to die is indeed gain. And this holds for the whole of us, the body of Christ, even more than for our individual lives. The body of Christ, Paul's dominant imagery for the church, is amplified by the figure of the bride of Christ, an ancillary symbolism. In both symbols the accent is on intimate sharing. What is closer than one's own body? With whom does a woman more suffusively identify than with her wedded spouse? And what these symbolisms say about the being of the church and the Christian works out through their doings. Daily, the actions and sufferings of Christians give force to their identity with Christ. Year by year, Christians find the Father of Jesus to be as He is with them (Exod. 3:14), the Spirit of Jesus to be like the master of their prayer, the human face of Jesus to be as their consoling companion, the life of Christ and the Trinity to be the inmost identity they are trying to realize, clarify, bring to fruition.

The Johannine notion of abiding in Jesus, or in the Spirit, or in the community of the three divine persons may be taken in the same direction. Like the Johannine figure of the branches that take their life from the vine, the abiding that Jesus invites (commands) is symbiotic: a sharing of life. If in the synoptic Gospels the disciples are invited to throw in their lot with Jesus, in John's Gospel they are invited to find their being in Jesus. From this it easily follows that they should share good times and bad, felicity and sorrow. Between them (us) and Jesus stands a community of interest. Everything that happens to the believer concerns Jesus. Not a hair of a believer's head (a hair of any child of God) falls without Jesus' Father knowing and caring. This may be hard to believe in hard times, when we are suffering injustices, but it is bedrock biblical faith. The line attributed to Job may be somewhat mistranslated, but it is completely consonant with Job's descent to radical faith: "Though he slay me, yet will I trust in him" (Job 13:15, KJV). In Jesus' words: "Not my will, but thine, be done" (Luke 22:42, KJV).

If we can take on even a small portion of these heroic dispositions, this carte blanche that the biblical God solicits, our prayer and problems of conscience greatly simplify. For prayer becomes as easy as talking over with God the ups and downs of each day, and problems of conscience have as their instinctive reference, "What would you do, God? How do these options square with the love I believe you are constantly trying to insinuate into my heart?" Such an instinctive reference does not absolve us from getting the relevant information, thinking through the likely consequences, or making unbiased judgments, but it places all these elements of good decision making before God as matters in which God too has a stake. When Saint Teresa said, "God and I are a majority," or the early Christians said, "It has seemed good to the Holy Spirit and to us" (Acts 15:28), they reflected such a sharing with God, such a situating of all decisions in the context of a prayerful intercourse with the Spirit.

## Heart Speaking to Heart

Prayerful intercourse with the Spirit, which is the Christian's most important ongoing formation of conscience, tends to develop into a heart-to-heart exchange. Just as a compatible husband and wife come to do much of their communicating with a glance, a pat, or a simple intuition, so do the Spirit and the devout Christian. To be sure, the equality that obtains in a good marriage is not possible with the divine Spirit. The Spirit always remains God the holy teacher, God the purest of guides. But the Spirit is also intimate, accepting, wholly identified with the causes of the devout believer. The Spirit encourages the believer to feel that nothing is foreign to the divine embrace, whatever is for the believer's good moves the Spirit's heart. This does not mean the sort of indulgence that would in the long run retard the believer's development. The Spirit will be as firm, as tough, as the believer's growth requires. But it does mean that the Spirit will make real the good news that God is on our side, salvation has been accomplished, by marrying into the believer's time, becoming the maestro who orchestrates the believer's prayer. In fact, I find it hard to overstress the gracious view that Paul sketches in Romans 8:

Likewise the Spirit helps us in our weakness; for we do not know how to pray as we ought, but the Spirit himself intercedes for us with sighs too deep for words. And he who searches the hearts of men knows what is the mind of the Spirit, because the Spirit intercedes for the saints according to the will of God. We know that in everything God works for good with those who love him, who are called according to his purpose.

—Romans 8:26–28

The image of the Spirit interceding for God's people, and so making them pleasing to the Father, conformed to the Father's will, makes plain the priority that orthodox Christian faith always gives to God's grace. We are free and responsible but God is always the initiator, ultimately the only adequate efficient cause, the only fully alluring final cause, who brings the work of salvation to fruition. In our deepest prayer, the Spirit speaks for us, God communes with God on our behalf. To enable this sort of prayer, we must offer the Spirit attentive hearts, still points of rational love, warm intelligences, that open to, abide with, the Mystery. The most transforming Christian prayer is a matter of letting the Spirit accomplish what the prophet Jeremiah long ago foresaw. Realizing that no simply literal observance of the covenant would do the job, Jeremiah envisioned an observance from the heart. In fact, he envisioned God's giving new hearts of flesh to the devout. Plucking out their old hearts of stone that had grown cold and no longer pulsed with religious love, the Lord would accomplish the intimate bonding desired. Then there would be little need for external teaching, for each person would know the Lord from within:

This is the covenant which I will make with the house of Israel after those days, says the Lord: I will put my law within them, and I will write it upon their hearts; and I will be their God, and they shall be my people. And no longer shall each man teach his neighbor and each his brother, saying, "Know the Lord," for they shall all know me, from the least of them to the greatest, says the Lord; for I will forgive their iniquity, and I will remember their sin no more.

—Jeremiah 31:33–34

A Johannine parallel to this inner transformation and instinctive knowledge of God occurs in the first epistle. Note that it is an overflow of the *abiding* in God that we have already stressed:

> Let what you heard from the beginning abide in you. If what you heard from the beginning abides in you, then you will abide in the Son and in the Father. And this is what he has promised us, eternal life. I write this to you about those who would deceive you; but the anointing which you received from him abides in you, and you have no need that anyone should teach you; as his anointing teaches you about everything, and is true, and is no lie, just as it has taught you, abide in him.
>
> —1 John 2:24–27

In his commentary on these powerful verses, Raymond Brown attributes their extremity to a controversy within the Johannine community. The author of the verses was trying to defend the faithful against false teachings, so he pushed for a nearly exclusive reliance on the Paraclete, who makes present the only absolute authority of Christian life, the teaching of Jesus himself:

> Nevertheless, in his opposition to false teaching the author goes to the extreme of denying the need of any teacher. Other NT works inculcate the need for authoritative teachers (I Tim 4:11: "Command and teach these things"), and indeed "prophets and teachers" were a regular feature in many churches (I Cor 12:28; Eph 4:11; Acts 13:1). Matthew 23:8 allows only Christ to be called a teacher, but I John's objection goes beyond the title. Since it is the anointing of the Christian that dispenses with the need for a teacher, the author is most likely basing himself on the promise of Jesus that the Paraclete would teach all things and guide the Johannine Christians along the way of all truth (John 14:26; 16:13). Behind that is the mentality that this is the "last hour" when direct divine guidance replaces human intermediaries. In Jeremiah's description of the New Covenant (31 [38]:34), which I have invoked as background several times, we hear, "No longer shall each man teach his neighbor and each his brother, saying, 'Know the Lord.'" And in John 6:45, the Johannine Jesus says, "It is written in the prophets, 'And they shall all be taught by God' [Isa 54:13]. Everyone who has heard the Father and learned from Him comes to me." . . . I

surveyed the range of teaching words in the Johannine literature, and by far the dominant usage pertains to Jesus. If the Paraclete teaches, it is because he takes over Jesus' role once Jesus leaves.[3]

The heart-to-heart quality of Christian prayer therefore is a strong complement to the outer teachings by which Christian consciences traditionally have been formed. It is no substitute for an immersion in doctrinal orthodoxy, but doctrinal orthodoxy without the inner anointing of the Spirit likely will be somewhat arid or inflexible. To know how the love of God would vivify a given situation, what the charity of Christ here and now is urging, we need to set our hearts in intimate converse with Christ's Paraclete.

## 8.

# CONTEMPLATIVE PRAYER

### *The Wholeness Love Stresses*

For Aristotle, who wrote the prime book of classical Western ethical theory, the *Nicomachean Ethics,* the norm of good action was what the *spoudaios* or mature person would do. Guided by *phronesis,* the virtue of prudential wisdom, the mature person would render justice, calculate probabilities, discern what was for the common good as well as any human agency could. Laws were good enough, but laws always depended upon a wise person to interpret or apply them. Only the *spoudaios,* tempered by experience, could be trusted to make a wise application. Ideally, in fact, laws would merely codify what the *spoudaios* had done, or would do, in such and such a situation.

Muslim ethics developed with much the same instinct. To supplement the Qur'an, which they conceived of as Allah's direct revelations to Muhammad, Muslim lawyers relied upon the *hadiths* or stories of how Muhammad had acted in such and such a situation. The Prophet was taken to be the prime Muslim, the best model of Islam, so whenever possible his practice supplied the norm. Muslim lawyers, like their Western counterparts, often fell into an arid concern only with

111

the letters. The notion of referring to a mature person's performative interpretation of the ideal more often than not fell into abeyance. But the intuition that matters of conscience, ethics, are only fully adequately handled by one who is imbued with the spirit of what the Muslim lifestyle is all about remained available to correct this amnesia, whenever Allah moved a wise person to the center of living faith.

One could draw analogies to other important ethical systems. Confucians, for example, had the example of the Master, who could say, when he had reached seventy, that the desires of his heart and the directives of the Way (Tao) of the ancients were one. Talmudic Jews could look to the teachings of the eminent rabbis, for whom Torah always was a vital Law, a guide they exemplified in their own lives. Christian moralists felt considerable pressure to correlate their prescriptions with the imitation of Christ that many generations placed at the center of Christian spirituality. Alternatively, they looked to the example of recent saints, whose free interpretations of doctrinal and moral orthodoxy brought the tradition alive, kept the anointing of the Spirit fresh.

The point should be clear enough. A well-formed Christian conscience is an understanding, an intelligence, a discerning sensitivity that enables one to deal with life in the round, nourishes one's growth into a holistic health. Religious maturity is not a process that goes forward unilaterally or linearly or according to legal charts. It is a circular or helical process, a going round and round the same problems, insights, preoccupations but at least at a slightly higher pitch, so that one gradually ascends to higher viewpoints, gains a stronger or more comprehensive grasp. Religious maturation is something organic, like the expansive growth of a tree. The healthy tree sends down deeper roots, sends up higher branches, and thickens at the trunk ring by ring. With time it becomes able to withstand greater stress, survive fiercer storms, grow fruit even in less than perfect soil or nourishment. It becomes solid enough to lean upon, supple enough to bend with the wind. To the writer looking out day by day from his little loft, it seems to grow more patient, more content to let its seasons unfold. The bright green leaves of spring have their beauty, but so do the thin, stark branches of winter. The lush foliage of summer is a pure blessing, but so are the colorful clothings of fall. For every time there is a purpose under heaven.

The mature conscience has a similar patience, and a similar holism.[1] It is a moral intelligence for the whole of life, all our seasons and all our zones of interest. Thus it is well to think of its formation as thorough rather than hurry up, deep rather than superficial, comprehensive rather than partial. Time was when this sort of formation would not have seemed strange, would only have paralleled the general education the young were receiving. Today one must stress the holism that the best formation of conscience demands, for the times have turned specialist, secular education has become truncated. When the measure of a student is what he or she can compute, studenthood has turned into malformation. Schools that won't stand against the pressures of the marketplace, won't insist on a dual preparation of their young people, for life as well as work, are a major part of our cultural problem.

Similarly, religious educators who don't realize that the church needs wise members more than technocrats or pragmatists badly disserve the body of Christ. The body of Christ is a community, an organism, of love. It will never flourish if left to lawyers or bureaucrats. There is a place for lawyers and bureaucrats, a variety of charisms, but neither law nor bureaucracy is close to being the most important charism. The most important charism is charity, without which there can be no religious wisdom, no insightful faith. For, as Bernard Lonergan has seen, faith is the knowledge born of religious love, the knowledge applicable to the whole of life because it stems from the heart of God's matter.[2]

## Appreciating Nature

When applied to Christian prayer, the wholeness that love stresses becomes a vote for contemplation. Contemplation is a prayer of simple regard, simple presence, simple loving. Flowing from the heart, the integral center, it loves to abide with the Mystery, gaze upon the icons of the Christ, commune heart-to-heart. Its delight is the Spirit's sighs too deep for words. Its nourishment is strange, subconceptual, a feeding that can occur almost unawares. In dark nights or clouds of unknowing, it makes real the theses about God's transcendence. From contending with God passionately, yet peacefully, it knows the truth of the traditional axiom that God is more unlike than like even our truest predications. Contemplation tends to become predominant, to take over the play in one's prayer, when sufficient familiarity with the ideas of Christian faith has rendered meditating on them unsatisfying. The person wants to love more than think, wants to commune more than reason. In the various species of contemplative prayer, this desire usually can find consolation.

Consider, for example, the lessons and satisfactions that lie ready to hand in the contemplation of nature. As the Psalms suggest, God has long been appreciated as the source of nature. Not only history, the realm of human experiences, lies under God's sovereign concern but also the processes of nature. Thus influential theologians such as Augustine have spoken of the things of nature, subhuman creatures, as vestiges of God. They are like footprints along the seashore, imprints of the One whose walk made space in the beginning. Today evolutionary theory makes this notion all the richer. The profusion of the species, their dynamic interactions and unfoldings, but magnify the creative splendor of God.

In their beauty and diversity, the flowers, fields, and animals paint the divine Creator as highly imaginative, wonderfully artistic. In their extent and silence, the swelling seas, craggy mountains, and trackless deserts suggest the awesome otherness of God. Even though we now can control many of nature's forces, the majesty of nature remains a source of perspective, a reminder of how tiny and fleeting we are. To the believer this reminder is another source of freedom. Where the unbeliever may find the vastness of the galaxies or the nearly incredible powers of the subatomic world further cause for considering humanity insignificant, the believer can make smallness a call to let fall the egocentricity that keeps her from surrendering to God, drop self-concern and put more of her time and energy into outgoing praise of God and service of neighbor.

In all these things we grope after a proper balance, but generally it is good for us to let go of our striving, our worrying, our planning. Most of us in the contemporary West are Pelagian rather than Quietist, people who err in the direction of self-reliance rather than in the direction of expecting too much of God. There are exceptions to this, of course, and it remains a daunting truth that God has set history into our hands. In matters military and economic, the disorders that our energetic messing around has caused cry out for energetic remedies. But in religious matters, matters of wisdom, our dominant sin more often is failing to pause, listen, appreciate.

Quietly, humbly, nature solicits our appreciation. True, at times nature grabs us by the scruff of the neck and forces our awe, even our fear, by a tornado, a flash flood, or a raging fire. But these are exceptional happenings, "acts of God" that insurance people place in a special category. It is the ordinary, daily busyness of the many species that is the more relevant contemplative focus. Each day the Creator sends mites out to do staggering amounts of work, produce gigantic numbers of descendants. The miles of root hairs a little patch of winter rye can grow, the millions of eggs a tiny insect can produce, rival the myriads of stars or Abraham's countless grains of sand beside the sea. If we would but read a couple of good naturalist books,[3] and then take ourselves to the window, or to the woods, or to the zoo, we would find dozens of new objects for religious contemplation.

To contemplate a natural object prayerfully, one need only quiet one's soul, focus one's senses, and let the object be framed by a sense of the Creator's presence. Then the yellow eyes of the lion will command a deeper respect, the Siberian tiger will prowl more provocatively. Then the empty landscape will tell of a God who is impersonal as well as personal, present in the rocks as well as the preachers. Driving around the Air Force Academy in Colorado Springs, in October when the rocks and trees coordinate superbly, I have felt my mind slip below ruminations about war and the preparation for war, youth and youth's future fate. The superb natural setting of the chapel of silver wings starts to offer consolations the chapel barely hints. There are forces greater than human wisdom and human folly, beings we may destroy but cannot create. Their creation, their simple brute being-there, is a primordial lesson we can never exhaust. Why are they, when they could never have been? What does their brute being-there say about the world and our place in it? Were we regularly to contemplate the mountains of Colorado, we would know most of the ecology the future is asking of us. Were we simply to attend, appreciate, let the scale and beauty of nature work on our spirits, we would rehabilitate enough awe and reverence to cure half our soul-sickness.

## Appreciating Other People

Nature qualifies as a genuine mystery, a pool of meaning too deep for our minds ever to fathom. The human person qualifies similarly: none of us has even plumbed the depths of another image of God. Contemplation loves to wait upon, to attend, genuine mysteries. The value of such attention in forming Christian consciences is that it stabilizes them in realism. If God, the ultimate Mystery, is to be the predominant reality in our lives (and so make our lives fully realistic or wise), we must regularly attend upon

God. If nature, other people, and our own selves are to be pregnant, pressed down and overflowing, as they should be, we must regularly attend upon them, appreciate their sacramentality. Jesus can only be the Christ, the anointed one who bears us God's kingdom, if we let the Spirit teach us the riches of the Incarnation. The Spirit can only be our Paraclete if we abide, watch, and pray. And the Father, the limitless resource whom Augustine likened to an infinite memory, going back and back, and whom Aquinas likened to an infinite act of understanding, blazing forth in all directions, can only be holy, mighty, immortal if we say "Our Father" in full passion, praise him ceaselessly with timbrel and lyre (Psalm 149:3).

In this section, though, the topic is other people, the neighbors we are to love as ourselves. If Jesus' ethics boils down to loving God wholeheartedly and loving neighbor as self, the present topic implies half a Christian ethics. It may initially suggest such humble foci as the person who works at the next desk, or the recalcitrant child who is a genius at getting our goat, but quickly it stretches forth implications of social justice, peacemaking, constraints on abortion, Christian politics, and much more.

The most radical social reformers are those who have seen their neighbors clearly, been moved to the quick by human misery. It is hard to imagine the programs of the biblical prophets without the widows and orphans who were being crushed, the Beatitudes of Jesus without the poor of Yahweh, the passions of Marx without the mills of industrial England.[4] This is neither to equate these three prophetic programs nor to close the door against other ways of fulfilling Jesus' second command. The mother spending herself for her family, the doctor laboring late into the night, the teacher living for the smallest victories over illiteracy may all be prodigal lovers of their neighbors. In their cases, too, a ray of light may one day have shone, the kaleidoscope one day have shifted and a beautiful pattern emerged, so that "neighbor as self" became as hard as a white pebble of the apocalyptic Christ, as warm as a fragment of heaven.

Humbler beginnings are safer, though, so let us contemplate a single small case. Once there swam into my ken a nearsighted woman who wanted to start a Women's Studies program. She was plain, bright, gentle, yet burning with a love of poetic truth, a need to dispel ignorance. In the happy days of her program's beginnings she enjoyed the respect, support, and faith of a wonderful college administrator. Under his patronage the project pecked its way out of its shell, smoothed its down, and started to take wing. Its timing was right so it attracted many young women confused about the sexual revolution, many older women struggling with unhappy marriages or going back to school. The woman didn't quite know what to make of her success. Her instinct was to spread the credit around, enlist as many people as possible in the governance of the program, think creatively about new ways to be of service. So there arose short-term workshops, community-oriented work-study projects, special courses on mothering, feminist leadership styles, and the like. Morale was high, women were flowering, and the school as a whole seemed to be taking on richer hues.

Then came the wintry storms. The supportive administrator left to take a better job (in part because he was tired of fighting the reactionaries). His replacement was an "old boy," on the record as opposed to innovative projects in general and Women's Studies in particular. These, he said, did not hew to the tried and tested ways of the established disciplines. They confused relevance with depth, interest with significance. Backed by an articulate herd of mastadons, who now felt free to trumpet their opposition to innovations (the old, championing administrator had largely kept them corralled), the new boss put the kibosh on any plans to expand Women's Studies. Benign neglect would be the stated policy, and the inner circle of program leaders heard hints that malignant attention might follow.

Contemplating the woman at this point, noting the droop of her shoulders and the lines across her brow, I thought of the Suffering Servant. At first the thought seemed inflated, grandiose, out of proportion. Later, on reflection, something in its intuition rang true. Here was an innocent, creative, well-intending agent of needed change being crushed by an insensitive, self-serving power structure. Here was a prophet being pilloried on the steps of the temple, as her forebears had been pilloried for centuries. Surely she was bearing the iniquities of us all, suffering for the redemption of the many. Surely God was blessing her pains beyond what she could know, seeing neath her stripes the bloodied body of Christ.

## *Appreciating Oneself*

Contemplations of our neighbors have the goal of sketching them on the model of Christ, bringing out their identification with the Head of the Body. Contemplations of the self can have the same goal. The more we appreciate our divine calling, the more likely we are to treasure our lives and gifts. The more we appreciate how we fail to put on the mind of Christ, grow into the measure of Christ, fill up the sufferings wanting to Christ, the more "sin" and "unprofitable servant" deepen in tone. We should love the selves that God sees, those sprightly, playful, responsive partakers of the divine nature. We should pity the sickly selves we too often glimpse in the mirror. We should try to distance ourselves from the hard, bitter, narcissistic selves that refuse to open to Christ's knock, want no part of the Spirit's cleansings. From our moments of peak consolation we should retrieve the self that might be, were God always blessing us with grace and we always receiving grace generously. From our times of deepest desolation we should keep at hand a sober humility, an awareness of how little we are on our own.

I remember walking beside a small pond in a New England woods and finding the self I had been looking for. It was fall, the air crisp, reds and yellows blazing from the trees. I had just heard a talk about three types of people. The first type would listen politely to the invitation of a generous leader and then turn away. The second would take the invitation to heart but prove to have no staying power. The third would leave all other concerns and wholeheartedly take up the cause of the leader. The talk was a recruitment into Christian service. To my late adolescent mind it made perfect sense. If someone made a serious proposal, and you found the proposal compelling, what could you reasonably do except accept the proposal and act upon it with all your heart? If Christ were proposing a campaign of the greatest moment, what believer could hear him and not be recruited?

My religious tradition did not speak much about rebirth, or being saved, or baptism in the Spirit. We had no mourners' bench or call to come forward and declare one's choice of Christ. Still, we did have a strong interest in religious vocations, and a keen realization that often such vocations declared themselves through inner crises or exceptional experiences. What surprised me, as I walked around the lake, my feet never lighter on the ground, was the sensibleness of what I was feeling. It seemed so obvious, the following of Christ, so logical and satisfying. If A (Christ's special status and clear call), and B (Christ's direction of his call to me), then C (my signing up) followed as surely as in any Aristotelian syllogism. At a stroke I could solve the problem of what to do with my life, which had started to become a burden. Only fifty years or so (if I lived the normal span) separated me from a complete success in heaven. Breathing deeply, I felt glad to be alive, content to have wrapped things up so tidily.

As things unfolded, of course, my life proved a little more interesting. But the core of the consoling experience, the sense of having been offered intimacy with God, service of God, gratuitously, for no merits of my own, as an utter mercy to a shabby sinner, remained. It proved both true and universal: When we were sinners,

God loved us. When we were callow and utterly naive, God beckoned us with a wry smile. And through all the unknowing we had to suffer—the pruning of our naiveté, the deflating of our complacency, the experience of the church's spots, wrinkles, and sins—the Spirit would replay the tape of our conversion experience, remind us of the grace of our calling. But this core proved capable of unexpected shifts in direction, unanticipated modes of application.

Thus, ten years after my promenade around the lake, I found myself walking the streets late at night, lost in the fog that often comes to wet Baltimore in the springtime, pondering what to do about a new love, how to square it with the earlier calling. It had come suddenly, this new seizure of my heart, on the swift wings of an interested glance of brown eyes across a party room. And it seemed doomed to frustration, strangled by differences in work, miles of distance. I wondered why it had happened, what it could possibly mean. I kept turning over the similarities between the core of what I felt now and what I had felt ten years previously, the analogy of the love experiences. Bruised from battering my head against a thick wall, sensing that I was becoming sick with frustration, I thought of biblical heroes who had hoped against hope, Tertullian and Kierkegaard who had believed because it was absurd. Abraham came to mind, dickering over Sodom and Gomorrah. Job stepped forth, muttering his complaints. I liked their style, their pluck, their refusal to let God escape involvement in their problems, responsibility for their fates.

And then, one day, things flipped over and I both let go and decided to act. It was very paradoxical, a shift in my continents, a new alignment of my subterranean masses. I would continue to be a follower of Christ (I hoped), a devotee of the only Mystery I'd ever found worth worshiping. But I would not be a man stripped of human needs, hushed of human hopes, alien to human tenderness. I would go for those brown eyes, enter Nietzsche's most dangerous combat, and leave the outcome, what happened to the warrior through the woman, in God's hands. I would, God help me, become a risker, a both/ander, a striver for knighthood of faith, with its impossible straddling of time and eternity. I would not ride a bullet train straight to heaven. I would go on pilgrimage, like most of humanity. And so it has been. The self I now contemplate is a pilgrim, a man under way.

## Silence and Unknowing

When the self finds an image that seems to epitomize its current state, it can leave off cogitating, try merely to attend. Placing the image against the backdrop of the Mystery, it can let the spiritual senses, the feelings of the heart, take the image into God's darkness, as a tacit petition for clarification, strengthening, conversion, or renewal. Christian contemplation becomes true prayer when the heart beats toward God in love. The implicit message of this beating is, "Do with me what you will, take my mess and salvage what you can, find something that will render you praise." Let us briefly ponder these tacit requests.

"Do with me what you will"—because I don't know what to do with myself. Twenty-five years after my calling I am more confused than ever. My first confusion was mainly a matter of unsettled desires and untutored intelligence. I had no notion of how my reason related to my emotions, where to look for my center. And I had no grasp of the Christian conception of reality, not the slightest sense of what the catechetical verities might mean experientially. So initiation and education proved immensely helpful. The future pilgrim at least learned how to read a map. Now the pilgrim wonders whether any map is long helpful, whether he is "going" any place we can chart. Yes, I have heard that the going is as important as the arriving, and I think I appreciate that truth. But I am confused more globally or radically, as though I were being turned this way and that like a swimmer under a huge wave. What is up, what is down, where is the light, where is the ground? Do with me what you will, God—for I don't know where to go, am lost in the deepening cloud.

"Take my mess and salvage what you can": I am as tumbled morally as intellectually, as untidy or imprecise in what I do and love as in what I think. Sometimes I do the good I want to do, feel the love I think I should. Sometimes the world seems nearly perfect, far too right for me to intrude. Other times I do nothing useful, seem cut off and without care. Other times the world seems clawed by unreason, nothing I could understand or join. The sin of the world clearly is my sin. We are siblings in our coldness and disorder. I fear that the embers of my passion are dying, my love is a mockery of "with whole mind, heart, soul, and strength." For the first time I understand Freud's death wish, the desert fathers' acedia, the tedium of life that the manuals discuss. So my consolation runs to lines like, "Even when our hearts condemn us, God is greater than our hearts," or "Nothing can separate us from the love of God." I can't salvage myself. I have no heart for the Sisyphean task of rolling my virtues up the hill, polishing my will like the witch's mirror. I must ask you, God, to be my salvager . . . God the junkman, the redeemer of wrecks.

"Find something that will render you praise": I do still want to give thanks, confess the divine beauties, render my praise. This is right and just, fitting as well as helpful to salvation. I can't deny the Trisagion, the seraphic "Holy, Holy, Holy." My biggest scrap of consolation is that I don't want to deny it, wish I could feel it as the seraphim do. That's now the thin wall between me and deep desolation, purifyings I would really fear. Yet to name it, remark it, is to wonder whether it too won't soon crumble, where the next hairpin turn will lead. Useless wondering. Presumptuous and mawkish thought. The profit to me in praise would be dropping such sentimentalities, focusing on God the other, God the pure. The profit to God in praise would no doubt be just what orthodox theology has always said: nothing at all. God needs my praise no more than God needs my being. I am, and I sing, only because God wanted to share the glory, to be "outside" as God is inside: loving and so generative, spirative, creative. Find something that will render you praise—because I don't find anything but a small still voice, a puny little want to pray.

These unknowings, as mangled and unattractive in their feeling as they are in their expression, make silence deeply attractive. The mess, the incompetence, the confusion all pressure me to get off the thought-track, the feeling level, and reconnoiter at the *apex animae,* the fine point of the soul. There space and time, reason and emotion, are much less oppressive. There a little word like *om* or *Christ* can do. This mantra is no magic. It is only a tiny toehold. Sometimes it helps me abide, endure, beat against the cloud. Sometimes it washes away in my distractions, is drowned in my self-concerns. Usually its going is both humiliating and radicalizing. I can't even depend on my own mind, my own wit, my own capacity to attend. I make God work through a maundering mind, a lustful, self-absorbed heart. I take God's call to carte blanche, abandonment, and make it the way not of the strongest but the weakest. Like a derelict trying to cadge a drink, putting out hands cracked bloody by cold and malnutrition, I play on the pity of God, act out the deadly truth that there is little health in me, little nature I have not abused. Then the Spirit sometimes takes pity, does what I ask, stops all my turmoil with peace. In silence, numbness of mind, opacity of desire, the Spirit lets me rest, ushers me into God's sabbath. And then I may remember how Jesus, the pioneer of our faith, inspired the author of Hebrews to write: "For we who have believed enter that rest" (4:3). I believe, Lord, help thou my unbelief.

___________ 9. ___________

# CASES AND AGENDA

*Cases of Bad Temper*

Like rain falling on a tin roof, so is the tattoo of a nagging spouse. Like the Chinese water torture, relentless and maddening, are the complaints and grumblings of too many of our fellow workers. By the time one has come of age, to meet a sweet disposition seems a blessing from on high. To deal with a person who looks toward the fair, accents the hopeful (without becoming a smile button), is to feel one has been gifted by the Spirit. Why does glumness or sourness afflict so many? What inner unhappiness or sense of injustice makes so many people overproducers of bile? These are the sorts of questions that moralists, those who would discourse on the formation of conscience, ought to give more attention. They are the sorts of questions that novelists often pose more intriguingly.

Consider, for example, the following description of a group of wealthy, successful businessmen:

How happy they might have been if they had recognized and gloried in their talent, confronting the world as gifted ego- tists, comparable to painters, musicians, or sculptors! But that was not their style. They insisted on degrading their tal- ent to the level of mere acquired knowledge and industry. They wanted to be thought of as wise in the ways of the world and astute in politics; they wanted to demonstrate in them-

125

selves what the ordinary fellow might be if he would learn to
think straight and be content to reap only where he had sown.
They and their wives (women who looked like parrots or bull-
dogs, most of them) were so humorless and . . . so cross that
I thought the ordinary fellow was lucky not to be like them.[1]

The businessmen are humorless and cross in good
part because they are unrealistic, constantly run afoul
of the way things are. In truth they owe their prosperity
to a rare talent for handling money. Something in this
repels them, however. It seems too crass or adven-
titious, so they reject the real reason for their prosperity
and go searching for reasons that will compile a more
flattering profile. Because they live in an era of history
(the late 1920s) and in a type of culture (WASP
Canadian) that above all prizes mercantile seriousness
(if only to offset the irresponsibilities of the jazz age and
the flappers), the profile most desired is that of an
industrious, weighty type who has his feet on the
ground, knows the ways of the world, and works like
Hercules. But they either are not this type, and have
prospered outside the straight and narrow path of clear
thinking and hard work (by illegalities, luck, or their
simple talent), or they know in their bones that this type
is a dullard, bound to lose in comparison with sunnier, if
less successful personalities. It is something like Luke's
contrast of the younger, prodigal son and the elder,
dutiful son in chapter 15. The elder son does all that he
is supposed to do, but with no flair, lightness, or grace.
The younger son messes up badly but somehow has
more humanity, more handles our sympathy can grab.
Other bad-tempered people seem to verify this
hypothesis of unrealism, or of wanting to be something
that is more desirable in talk than in its actual
possession. The local grump paints himself as a long-
suffering victim. The work he does is not appreciated—
because it serves such lofty standards. The students he
teaches are unworthy of him—because they cannot be
as "rigorous" as he about the subject he teaches. The
ironies in this situation completely escape him. The
lack of self-knowledge that makes his psyche limp
would be mitigated by half were he to take lightly

William James's theses about the religion of sick souls, any good teacher's memories of wayward student days. But he will not or cannot, so he grumps and bellyaches and generally makes himself a nuisance. It is a way of gaining attention, arrogating power, putting a sign on his door that he is formidable.

I suppose that's the special noxiousness of a bad temper: the ease with which it becomes a calculated means to dominance. The curmudgeon and the shrew meet so few people who will stand up to them, tell them to take a hike, that they gain considerable leverage. Most people tiptoe around their little preserves as though they were the lairs of bears. Children stifle their giggles, peers bow and defer—all to avoid the upsetting blowup, the storm of thunder and lightning. I myself think that this is a shortsighted cowardice, a connivance in the person's sickness. But there is no denying that life is hard enough without having to deal with X's bitter tirades, Y's sullen sulks. Many of us live close to the end of our ropes, our energy and patience already overdrawn. So we avoid any draining, tumultuous battle we can. Now and then we take a stand—when not to do so would be completely irresponsible. Most days, though, we trim to the wind, let the grump have his way.

What the grump seldom realizes, however, is that getting his way will only take him another step from his goal. His goal, perversely enough, usually is not the power or influence that even the casual observer can see him winning. It is esteem, admiration, affection, even love. Crabs are like the rest of us in wanting to be affirmed (if anything, they are hungry for more affirmation). But the means they choose to express this need are 180 degrees wrong. So they win but more significantly lose, gain some power but lose more sympathy. So they find affirmation and love receding on the horizon, their lives becoming ever more frustrating and lonely. It is a cruel fate to become a crotchety crab, a species of damnation.

The bad-tempered person considers the world an enemy, and so closes to much of its light. The sweetness of the Spirit is beyond him, so he says that sourness is realism. As a result, peace and joy seem chimeras, the dictum of Hobbes becomes gospel: "People treat one another like wolves." When a conscience accepts such a jungle law, it becomes hard put even to restrain itself to an eye for an eye. Thinking that most folk are its enemies, it contemplates first strikes, preemptive actions, that would take the other wolf's eye before its own is imperiled. Then we have the siege mentality of our contemporary nuclear age, in which the destructiveness of our weaponry, combined with the paranoia of too many citizens, gives any person of common sense cold sweats.

## Cases of Sexual Disquiet

Most cases of bad temper, of course, occur at some remove from the nuclear trigger. It is the neighborhood cream they curdle, life in the small. The same with most cases of sexual disquiet. If the perversions of the high and mighty make the scandal sheets at the checkout counters, the disorders of local small fry do most of the grass-roots damage. As with bad temper, sexual disquiet is both a social disease and a personal menace. Closing the soul to God's holy mystery, muddying the waters so that the Spirit cannot be discerned, it warps the relations between men and women, throws all sorts of people out of joint. What should be a source of energy, joy, and good humor becomes something sleazy and furtive. What should be strong and bouncy becomes bumped and ground. Faces that could shine with joy become clouded with shame (or brazen with shamelessness). Trust frays here, there, around the corner until the social fabric wears thin. In most communities, not even the church is exempt from sexual disquiet.

In the male scenario that regularly plays in my neighborhood, something starts simmering around thirty and by forty often blows up. Whether one calls it boredom, failed dreams, or a fear of aging and impotence, it almost always bespeaks a distance from God, a lack of frank prayer. The man is unable to be the self he had projected—rich, famous, powerful, a great lover, or whatever—and he does not know what to do with his supposed underachievement. Because he has lived most of his years on the surface, a stranger to his emotions and depths, he has few resources for coping with his malaise. He knows nothing about consolation and desolation, so he cannot discern the spirits. He hasn't read or intuited the patterns of the life cycle, so he doesn't know about "typical" crises. His culture constantly lures him with sexual phantasies, saying that any satisfying life is swinging. He has no guru stronger than his newspaper and television, no testament that he ponders as the wisdom of the ages.

It is tragicomic, this regular male pattern, yet more serious than the flings of youth. These do their damages, of course, but some of youth's disquiets are the obvious product of a clash between physical maturity and the social or psychological immaturity that the long education demanded in our culture allows. The tragic side is the damage done to wives, children, the self, and the community at large. The comic side is the rationalizations and posturings that come forth: going for the gusto, saying why not jewelry and perfume for men? If the comedy comes to predominate, so that the man can laugh at his foolishness, therapy is well under way. If the rationalizations harden and erotic fulfillment becomes something encoded in the Bill of Rights, the man is a hard case, something the Spirit is not likely to crack without heavy pounding.

The female scenario that I see is more complicated, perhaps because I can't know it from within. In my experience, in most of the marital breakups whose overt cause is infidelity, the offender is the male. What lies behind this offense, in terms of general tensions or specifically sexual dissatisfactions, I know only in the few cases where I have become a counselor. There the woman's sexual needs have been more diffuse or global than the man's, capable of fulfillment as much through broad affection as through narrow intercourse. Even the few women initiating marital breakups, or stalking as predatory singles, seem to suffer from a diffuse disquiet, in which physical sex plays only a relatively small part. Work, self-esteem, and a sense of becoming their own person loom larger.

These women cannot put up with the assumptions and insensitivities that many of their mothers did, have been rubbed raw by the changes of the last fifteen years and feel women's subjugations keenly. Now and then a truly promiscuous woman seems to care little about the personality of the man with whom she is involved. But this is far less common than the woman who is confused, bitter, and alienated from a church that she thinks has colluded in her suppression. She wants a relationship that will be respectful of her needs, make her as free as the man, take sex as but one important piece in a considerably larger puzzle. She wants—did she but know it—the sort of health that the Spirit has long promised but many ecclesiastical mediators of the Spirit have not known. I always feel a special pang for such women (and men): had we more authentic churches they would be many fewer and their sufferings would be much less.

## The Problem of Money

Bad temper and sexual disquiet taint the human spirit and so frustrate the work of the divine Spirit. Like a noxious red dye, they make the person polluted, dangerous, in need of strong antidotes. The problem of money has a similarly grim potential. If a person becomes avaricious, greedy, obsessed with lucre, lucre turns filthy and fouling. The classical Chinese spoke of the three great life-cycle struggles as fighting lust when one is young, fighting strife when one is middle-aged, and fighting greed when one is elderly.[2] This suggests that those coming in sight of death may try to distract themselves, or block out their sense of diminishment, by piling up fat bank accounts or amassing precious possessions.

Whatever the psychological and religious causes, the effects of greed are destructive and unattractive. Misers, as many classical literatures have portrayed them, are mean, constricted types, lacking something essential to healthy humanity. The hospitality that ancient cultures emphasized, in which a host outdid himself to be generous to his guest, was not only a way of coping with life on the road in an age of no motels. It was also a way of combatting possessiveness, fighting the tendency to value material riches more than human beings.

That is the crux of the economic disorders that rightly draw religious criticism today: the majority of the world's systems seem tempted (to say the least) to value profits more than people. The large-scale swindles and corporational callousnesses we see in our own country may pale in comparison with the disregard of human welfare that abounds in totalitarian and military regimes, but it is still a gross and cancerous set of sins. No one ought to have insufficient food, clothing, shelter, education, and health care in the United States. For a country as prosperous as ours to have thirty million at the poverty level or below mocks our pretensions to religion. You cannot love the God you do not see if you don't love (practically, effectively) the neighbor staring you in the face. You can't claim brotherhood, sisterhood, with people of all races and have the statistics we have on black unemployment. A people that valued human welfare more than material luxuries could solve the worst sufferings of its poor in a year. With a will to make the superfluous wealth of the upper classes over to those who lack life's necessities, and then a simple and fair tax structure, we could cure legions of sufferers. The situation might be different in other countries, on other continents, but in North America and Europe there is no excuse.

Similarly, there is no excuse for unemployment, if one has taken Jesus' message to heart. Society has plenty of good work that needs doing. In education, health care, basic science, appropriate technology (E. F. Schumacher's technology that is small scale and meets peoples' local needs[3]), drug rehabilitation, and the like we could well use millions more workers. The basic obstacle to full employment is the same as the basic obstacle to eliminating poverty: the unwillingness of our citizenry at large to live frugally, with little superfluity. Driven by advertising and the profit motive, we have convinced ourselves that our economy must ever grow, bigness is necessary. Even apart from the economic devastation wreaked by our expenditures for defense, which basically are unproductive (return nothing useful to the system except a certain dubious security), the major assumptions of our peacetime economy run counter to Christian instinct. For Christian instinct gives anything extra to neighbors in need, because neighbors are other selves. Christian instinct fears wealth, because the Lord said that it is easier for a camel to pass through the eye of a needle than for a rich person to enter the kingdom of God. Christian instinct thinks that a person who stores barns full of treasure and bids her soul wax fat is risking the Lord's wrathful verdict: "Fool! This night your soul is required of you; and the things you have prepared, whose will they be?" (Luke 12:20).

There are, of course, things that belong to Caesar, the secular realm, and money is one of them. There are good uses for money: subsistence, charity, the support of science and art. In Christian perspective money is simply a means. It is as good or bad as the uses to which it is put. By observation, however, one sees that it tends to distort many lives, either because people pursue it too assiduously (and so neglect the more important things of the soul), or because people use it badly, for self-promotion rather than social service. The branch of Christian churchdom that equates financial prosperity with virtue, thinks that doing well in the stock market is a mirror of doing well in heaven, would be laughable were it not so fertile in sin. If there is anything that the New Testament makes plain, it is that Jesus lived freely, with little concern for material securities, devoured by his service of God and neighbor. He associated much more with the poor than the rich, identified much more with the have-nots than with the powerful.

Thus a conscience formed to the pattern of Jesus will

always find secular living irrational and distorted, especially in its great concern with money. I live in a pocket of the country where "entrepreneurship" recently has become a sacred mantra, so I especially hate the pious distortions of bankers, the cant of fast-food franchisers. They would measure each person's net worth in dollars. In my town, to be on the make is to expect praise as a new missionary. But greed and entrepreneurial hustle manifestly are not enough, manifestly soon turn dysfunctional and exacerbate the problem. As the Israelite prophets wanted mercy rather than sacrifice, so we should want generous compassion rather than ruthless hustle, a system that does justice to the many rather than a system that pimps for the few. The problem of money is imbalance, injustice. Money is the root of too many evils for the wise person not to judge it harshly.

## The Problem of Power

Those who pursue or use money in a disordered fashion tend to target it for luxuries or power. They want the good things of life, the things that turn body and soul sleek, or they want special influence over other people. Many of the people who listen to contemporary advertising yearn for gourmet meals, plush carpets, designer clothes, and membership in the country club. When a stockbroker gives out special tips, many of the people who pay attention want to be king of the hill, queen of the hive. These people know that the bigger their pile, the more their resources for buying power. For some of them power will become the great aphrodisiac, the way they get their jollies. Then vanity, pride, and even sadism beckon on the horizon. By the time power has become eros God beholds a quite sick soul.

For the truth, of course, is that all power tempts to amnesia. Lord Acton's dictum ("power corrupts") needs this refinement if it is to serve in Christian analyses. Power need not corrupt (it does tend to corrupt); the corruption most likely is a rotting of memory, an eating away of confessed creaturehood and so bedrock humility and realism. Everything that we are and have depends upon God: that is the Christian bottom line. Any power (as any wealth or talent) that we gain comes from God and ought to be used for service. Yes, the sweat and toil by which we polish talent can be praiseworthy. Humanly speaking, the work that can go into acquiring wealth or power can be impressive. But the whole scenario is askew, from the viewpoint of faith, unless one's power becomes the uncoercive, servant force of love. The healthy believer never forgets that the power of the Christ became manifest in his weakness. It was by dying on the cross that Christ destroyed sin and death. It was on the cross that Christ demonstrated the ultimate power of love.

So the problem of power settles into proportions, alignments, quite like those of the problem of money. Power is problematic because we find (as a matter of empirical observation) that many people handle power badly, we ourselves often cannot keep it in balance. This is true of military power, as America's recent excursions, from Vietnam to Lebanon and Grenada, clearly show. It is true of political power, as the *Congressional Record* for any year would report. And, most unfortunately, it is true of church power.

Of all the institutional powers, the ecclesiastical has the clearest call to be servant. Therefore its corruptions are especially contrary to God's will, especially wounding to Christ's body. There are the corruptions for the sake of worldly influence and luxury. There are the corruptions that ally themselves with legalism, to protect the status quo. And there are, as the most widespread corruptions of all, the insensitivities that come when people get accustomed to ruling the consciences of others, passing moral judgments and saying they know better. We never know better than the Holy Spirit. We always have the obligation to hear what the Spirit is saying to the Seven Churches. Look at many of our denominations' records on controversial issues of our time. Can any honest person say that power hasn't greatly corrupted some of these decisions? Look at the simple faithful who have been ground under by the big bureaucracies. Can any sensitive person's gorge not rise? This is not to deny many wonderful services and wonderful people in many of our churches. It is not to say that all of our churches have always made bad decisions. It is just to say that the lessons about power read out to the Gentiles have an embarrassing relevance at home. We do well to keep First Peter 4:17 as a mezuzah above our lintels, a constant reminder on our walls: "For the time has come for judgment to begin with the household of God."

I have sometimes functioned as one of my church's powerholders, and those times have bequeathed me an enduring unease. The spiritual power that a religious community grants its ministers can be a wonderful thing, opening people to healings and inspirations they might otherwise never know. But it can also take on a life of its own, a bent detrimental to the work of the Spirit. Roles can eat up people. Sexual energies can play masked parts. The sonorities of voice and performance can sport on their own. Even the best-intentioned praise can complicate the church's prophetic task, as even the best-meant consolations can veil the sufferer or penitent from the Spirit. Most of this complication is bondage we cannot avoid, the price we pay for not being angels, beings pure and simple. We could chasten and defang most of it, though, were we to insist on greater spirituality.

In worship ceremonies, for example, we could make it plainer than often we do that the praise of God is the sole reason-to-be. Neither the music, nor the sermon, nor the socializing are ends in themselves. All are but means to the praise of God. In spiritual direction we could make it plainer than often we do that the way of the mature is not sweet, let alone cloying. As soon as we can bear it, the Father starts scraping away our pride, refining our realism, as Christ promised in John 15:2: "Every branch of mine that bears no fruit, he takes away, and every branch that does bear fruit he prunes, that it may bear more fruit." I don't mean, of course, that we should be harsh or cruel. I don't mean that the Spirit doesn't console us and ministers ought not be gentle. I just mean that the power of God soars as far from our self-service as the heavens from the earth, that the consuming power of God is love rather than dominion.

## The Inevitability of Politics

In trying to mature consciences to love rather than dominion, service of the poor rather than adulation of the wealthy, self-control rather than sexual looseness, and good humor rather than bad temper, we are always dealing with people who are social beings, political animals through and through. Communal existence is as integral to human beings as having an upright carriage, a dexterous thumb, language, or any of our other specifying traits. When religion blinks this truth, forms consciences as though people were isolated monads, it condemns itself to irrelevance. When it does not get a firm fix on the special brand of politics that Christian faith implies, it further botches the job. So high on the agenda of any discerning set of reflections on Christian conscience is the inevitability of politics, the call to carry the gospel into the polis.[4]

For Thomas à Kempis, who felt that he always came back from the polis less a man, the inevitability of politics was dolorous. Thomas found that a well-kept monastic cell soon turned sweet, forays into the external world were distracting. Defining the Christian ideal in terms of a recollected consciousness focused on the imitation of Christ, he had little time or place for the buyings and sellings, butcherings and bakings, that preoccupied most of his contemporaries. These preoccupations had the great liability of making people forget death, the ominous enemy that only recollected living can turn into a friend. When we don't fly away into busyness, do abide and keep watch, death makes life serious, gives each day a sharp point. The wise virgins always keep their lamps trimmed, for they know that the bridegroom may appear at any moment. The worldlings forget and let their lamps burn low. Politics should never become so absorbing, the contemporary adapter of Thomas might say, that the great verities of sin and death, grace and resurrection, no longer define our reality.

Granted that, politics can make a good response to its other venerable accusers, such as Tertullian and Jerome, who asked what Athens has to do with Jerusalem. Athens, the symbol of humanistic learning, has everything to do with Jerusalem, the city of the Christ, if the Christ is God's Word incarnate, the entry of God's speech into flesh. Let Christian theology simply be orthodox and a Christian humanism is inevitable. The Word of God has touched every bit of human existence, since human existence is part of a dynamic concatenation of beings, salvation is utterly ecological. In the wake of the Christ the motto of the Roman poet Terence can become a white pebble of Christian conviction: "I think that nothing human is foreign to me." Through its sacramental system, the church has lived out the core of this conviction. In its art, iconography, educational and medical endeavors, it has depended on the Lord's tent being pitched in our midst. So too in its politics. For all the soiling and sullying that the church's dalliances with the secular powers have brought, the church's interactions with the secular powers have been inevitable.

I find no brief, then, for a Christian secession from politics. Within the church universal there may be an important role for those who fear capitulation to the world's dark powers, but the secessionist mentality reveals an appalling lack of faith in the Christian doctrines of creation, incarnation, and redemption. If we follow Paul, where sin abounded, grace has abounded the more. If we follow John, the Word that was with God in the beginning was God, became flesh and came unto God's own. Even when the consciences of God's own condemn them, say that they did not receive their Savior or know the things for their peace,

Jesus' God is greater than their hearts, and God alone knows all. So while the charitable works of many sectarian groups in my area win buckets of points for their heritage, the bitter paranoia of many other sectarians in my area take most of those points away, placing the heritage in heavy brackets. God so loved the world that he gave his only begotten Son. The Son's followers cannot hate the world without contradicting what their leader was all about.

It is right and just, proper and helpful to salvation, therefore, to stand foursquare in the world and help to shoulder its political burdens. On the other hand, it is only fully Christian to do this with a view to opening the world to the grace that alone can heal and fulfill it. How to do this without being pious or simpleminded is a nice question. Certainly the Christian politician, professional or amateur, needs a better education than what many who now claim that name display. In them one sees no lovely symmetry between the orders of nature and grace, no translation into political terms of the notion that grace perfects nature. Equally, one sees no sharp sense of the antagonism that can arise between nature and grace when "nature" comes to think that sin is one of its essential parts. The irrationality and lovelessness of sin are no essential parts of human nature. Sin is nothing positive, intelligible, or creative in itself. So while politics must always reckon with sin, it can never justify sin by accepting it as normalcy.

I find this catholic Christian instinct sorely lacking in many policy discussions about war making, ecological pollution, abortion, and the like. Military service, for instance, can be commendable, but militarism can never be. In my opinion, defending the victims of abortion can be commendable, but defending the act itself can virtually never be. Acknowledging that ecological pollution is complex is sheer realism, while justifying ecological pollution is but further sin. For the Christian, faith inevitably makes hard political problems still harder, all the while that it clarifies those problems' best solutions.

# SUMMARY

### Why to Examine One's Conscience

We have circled around several aspects of Christian conscience, stressing the reflective, judgmental processes by which most of its maturation occurs, and trying to suggest how these processes meld into the discernment of spirits and contemplative prayer. Where possible we have taken up concrete examples and dealt with case studies. The entire effort has been to evoke what the maturing Christian conscience looks and feels like. What kinds of activities do adult Christians, serious about their faith, engage in when they want to clarify their moral sensibilities? What are the biblical phrases, traditional exercises, or contemporary trends that they find themselves probing?

In my view we best conceive Christian conscience by placing it in the context of the life of grace that inserts us into God's redemptive order. Further, I think that we best mature a Christian conscience by a regular regime of reflection, the key focus of which is a prayerful check on our obedience to Jesus' twofold command. If we are trying to love God wholeheartedly, especially by a daily contemplative prayer that takes grace to mean a marital relation with God, we are alive to the import of Jesus' own center, his passionate relation to his Father. And if we are trying to do justice to our neighbors, to carry into the worlds of work, politics, and socializing the love of God that we beg in our prayer, then we have not forgotten Jesus' second commandment and still can bear the judgment scene in Matthew 25, where the sheep separate from the goats on the question of practical love of neighbor.

To summarize these intertwined convictions, let us focus on the examination of conscience, reviewing both its why and its how. Why the examination of conscience? Because this staple of traditional Christian spirituality puts a very practical point on the theology and ethics of faith. The person who checks her standing with God each day, not in the manner of a greedy bookkeeper but with a lover's desire to please, has a simple yet flexible and effective way of living out her faith. If morning and/or evening she takes the time to center down, check the patterns of her recent experience, and offer what she finds to God (Father, Son, or Spirit), her life will soon become regularized, her marriage with the Lamb bear fruit. Our connection to God doesn't strengthen, mature, gain greater richness and nuance automatically. We have to put conscious effort into this love relation just as with any other.

Yet so little a daily contact as fifteen minutes of absolutely honest conversation each morning can keep the bond well tied, make the Spirit our most significant silent partner. Then the Mystery that grounds all people's lives can become in our life the fullness of Christ's love. Then the purposelessness that debilitates so many of our contemporaries regularly will get a stiff counterpunch. Daily examination of conscience will not, of course, remove all our problems. In some ways it will complicate or increase the stakes of our lives. But now and then it will become the means through which God will wipe every tear from our eyes. Now and then it will remind us of the pearl of great price, the joy held out, and so enable us to suffer the cross. How, when, or where this will happen no one can say. But that it will happen is the regular testimony of all the saints who have persevered, as well as the obvious implication of the promise that God's grace will be sufficient.

The examination of conscience, then, has an appealing neatness. It is a way of assuring, at a single stroke, that we involve ourselves with the processes that keep faith alive, keep us abiding in the love life of the Trinity. It also has an attractive (and daunting) depth. Because its tendency is to shorten the review of our moral assets and liabilities, and lengthen our communion with God, the examination easily becomes the framework for a deepening contemplation. This is quite ordinary, nothing mystical or giving cause for pride. Just as our relations with a good friend or spouse tend to simplify, as we come to know one another well enough to skip the dozen explanations a stranger would need, so our relations with the Spirit tend to simplify. Through our day by day exchanges we learn that the Spirit is the master, no time or experience is irrelevant or unredeemable, the only way to repay God is with a blank check. If we have sinned, we can go to the Spirit for forgiveness. If we have done well, we can go to the Spirit to share the good news. The Spirit wants to participate in all our works, all our friendships. The Spirit wants to defend us against all our foes. We are not alone, if we meet the Spirit each morning. Even to search for the Spirit each morning is to learn the truth, the simple realism, of Jesus' promise that he would not leave us orphans.

Without a daily search for God, we are indeed alone, do face the world as orphans. And among the varieties of such searches the examination has the advantage of being utterly practical, completely attuned to what our love relation with God is or is not doing to our kids, on the job, at the church. Mature Christian consciences do not separate prayer and work, contemplation and action. Mature Christian consciences know that God wants, encourages, enables a whole offering, a complete union. That is why they tend to check in with God each day.

## How to Examine One's Conscience

The how of the examination of conscience is as simple as reflection, and the many pages we have spent on reflection should have made it clear that we need only pause and review to begin to get in touch with what has been happening to us, start reading the signs of our times.[1] Consider, for example, Joe, a young father-to-be, who regularly rises while the day is fresh and gives himself a half hour on the back porch for reflection. When he muses about how things are going this day he finds that he is both excited about the coming birth and a little afraid. Cathy has had wonderful health throughout the whole pregnancy, but there is always the chance something could go wrong. Looking at this fear, he finds he can only turn it over to God: "It's probably foolish, I know. But please take special care of her. Bring this wonderful thing you've begun to a good conclusion. Let it go well. Let her feel the joy of bringing forth new life, all the sense of mystery." Joe can say this simply, almost imperatively, because his communion with God is regular, habitual. Not only does he faithfully keep his morning half hour, through the day he gets reminders of God's interest. Slowly, without a lot of effort on his part, more ups and downs suggest asking God's help or giving God thanks.

Joe is also afraid of the changes that the new baby is likely to bring. This is a light fear, nothing very weighty. In fact, many prospective fathers might not even notice it. But his examinations have sensitized Joe to little pangs of jealousy in himself, times when the baby has seemed to crowd him out. He has made fun of these pangs, both to Cathy and in his prayer. That's been a good way to cope with his regrets at leaving the private world of their twosome, and with his even subtler pangs that Cathy seems much less regretful. Her parenthood is more natural than his, something she appears little to worry. He feels a bit superannuated, as though thirty-three were too old to be starting this business. The four years they've been married have been the happiest of his life. Will the baby change that? Shouldn't he be taking this question to God?

"I want to go forward, God, and I am going forward happily enough. But you see my little hesitations, my reluctance to cross into new territory. Help me to give up our privacy more gracefully, and not to burden Cathy with things she doesn't fear. Help me realize the dangers of holding back, the suffocations and sterilities. I know about generativity, the need to be fruitful, at least on the level of theory. I've read the books and felt the feelings. But in practice it's more complicated. Help me to let go, give over, go with the drift of my time. A child is a big responsibility, but also such a blessing. I'll probably learn things about myself, and about you, that I never would have guessed. Most people would be so happy they'd have no time for such pesky little worries. Let my thank-you's outweigh my help-me's. Let me emphasize the gift and downplay the price."

These are the main things on Joe's mind this morning. Nothing else raises its head. His work and his relations with Cathy are running smoothly. The things on his immediate schedule pose no special problems. So he uses the last part of his examination to contemplate God in the new day, the fresh breeze caressing the porch. Wordlessly, with simple heartbeats of affection, he tries to express his appreciation for being alive in such a beautiful world, being immersed in creation and birth. May the Christ who makes these graces be ever blessed. May the Spirit of love who keeps them glowing be ever praised. May the Father of Lights from whom all good gifts descend ever be hallowed. These are phrases that pop through Joe's mind, shaping his simple communion. They are bits of imagery molding his spirit, and they send him forth in gratitude. Other days he might finish his examination, take breakfast to Cathy, and drive off in a darker mood, still trying to reconcile himself to the headlines, still pondering new evidences of hatred and sin. Today his exiting mood is peaceful and expectant. His anxieties about the birth have abated. Today the Spirit has left him calm and joyous. That is how the Spirit often leaves him, and why he seldom misses his morning half hour.

Joe and others who run down their consciences before God regularly tend gradually to simplify the procedure. Now and then they make a formal inventory of the big questions in their lives, but most days they simply quiet their minds, attend to their feelings, and find a few relatively small-scale matters begging attention. Not all days are as easy as the one we have observed. Many days the worries are greater, more objective and weighty. But even bigger worries are cut down to size, no longer seem bogies, when we set them against God's mystery. God is great and most of our human concerns are quite small. God is alpha and omega, high and low; our human affairs are at best middling. Yet, middling or massive, everything directs the mature conscience to God. Great matters of war and justice immediately beg God's wisdom. Little matters of making it through the day become playful parts of the divine comedy, tiny colors in the great tapestry.

## Maturation in Prayer

Prayer matures by deepening our immersion in the mysteries of God and God's plan. It takes us more profoundly into the love of God and so brightens our faith, makes Jesus and the biblical realities more objective. With time we begin to take the global, opaque presence of God for granted, according it an objective status like that we accord the sky, the air, our constant-yet-ever-changing neighborhood. In God we live and move and have our being. God is more marvelous than the gold-streaked sky, the child's solemn big eyes. In his own order God must also be more concrete and exact. Yet our order is too limited to define God this way, too finite and sinful. So in our order God often is cloudy, nightlike, a Spirit breathing at will. God's son would be as physical for us as our bodies, our wine and bread, were we to see face to face, know as we are known. But now we see through a glass darkly, move by faith and hope. Now we try to love, pray always, and in patience possess our souls. God's glory is far above us. We have sinned and fallen far short. But God, who has already laid sin waste and made death captive, will come to work wonders beyond all our sin.

God knows how to make sense of these bits and pieces of revelation. Prayer turns them over and lets them go, returning to a few well-worn images, phrases, feelings, or corners of dark peace like the tongue to a sore tooth. Some days prayer is absolutely minimal: a resentful body taking its chair, a mind dry and rebellious. Other days prayer is easy and obvious: How is it going, my love? But in maturity all days are prayerful. For better or worse, richer or poorer, in sickness and health, God has us until death parts the last barrier and we consummate our long longing. Mature prayer thinks of itself as paying with an old and battered blank check. Even though each payment increases its debt, it keeps pushing its dog-eared mite forward. For it knows, dimly but adequately, that progress is deeper indebtedness. If everything is grace, any better perception means more laud of God, greater abasement of self. So the Baptist's formula: He must increase, I must decrease. So the constant liturgical refrain: Praise God!

The brilliant side of prayer-thought, the pirouettes and tricky tropes, is not untrue, but it tends to be less useful than the pedestrian terra firma. Clod by clod, we members of the body of Christ must remember that we are but dust and unto dust we shall return. Sin by sin, we must learn that Adam's fault was happy. In the topsy-turvy world illumined by conversion, everything magnifies God. Though God forbid that we should sin in order to exalt the divine mercy, the divine mercy is exalted in each recognition of sin. Though we are unprofitable servants, God's design is realized each time we confess our helplessness. God's design is love, God's giving and our receiving. God's paradigm is Christ, what happens when love given meets love received. Christ is the more angular, individual, cranky, gentle, poetic for surrendering himself to the Mystery. The most mature of us all, the freest and most energetic, had no will of his own, was fully obedient to the Father. So the mind dances, spins, tries to mount the helix and then packs it into the heart. What defeats the mind can please the heart, for the heart has reasons the mind knows not. This does not make faith irrational. It blesses no superstition or sappy credulity. It simply bids the mind stop babbling, bids the senses quiet down. "Let the whole self do its best thing," it says. "Let it watch and abide."

Mature prayer watches and abides. Mature prayer therefore is not difficult to conceive, no esoteric affair reserved for the few. Anyone not having always to blather can pray quite maturely. Anyone continent in mind and emotion can open to the Spirit. The Spirit can't do much for people who aren't "there," scatter themselves hither and yon. There are mercies for such people, of course, and they never fall beyond God's pale. But they are like obstreperous children, very difficult to teach. So sometimes the Spirit smacks them, to force a little attention. Sometimes we only listen because we are heartsore. If Jesus learned obedience through suffering, the rest of us likely will bleed.

In maturity we don't mind bleeding all that much. We're gnarled and scarred anyway, so what are a few more gashes? It's embarrassing that the bulk of our suffering continues to stem from our own foolishness. We blush the worse for still being so thick. But, as grotesquely as Popeye, we are what we are. God loves what we are. God would like us to be better, but only so that God could love us more effectively, consolingly. If suffering will lower our barriers, break down our pride and pretense, God will let suffering rip. The explosions of the stars and the gore of evolution show that God is no satin Pollyanna. God can be as cruel as the cross, as angry as hell, when love and sin so conspire.

Still, every instinct of faith says that God does nothing except from love. And every logical entailment of this proposition leads back to the blank check. The only warrant for abandoning ourselves to God is God, but this makes faith utterly reasonable. Indeed, now and then, when we are touched by the divine exchanges of the Trinity, the completely mutual surrenderings of light, life, and love, faith seems completely obvious, wholly unavoidable. But most days our dark glass doesn't show this. Only the saints get a steady glimmer.

In itself, they say, it is as plain as Christ's cross, as vivid as Christ's glory. For the 144,000 hymning the nuptials of the Lamb, it must be as big as life.

## Maturation in Politics

Many days maturation in politics (gaining a view of the social nature of human beings that rings consonant with Christian love) sketches itself as a realistic assessment of human cooperation, a sensible expectation of one's neighbors. What, in all fact and prudence, can we expect from the people at work, the people in our town, our fellow Americans, our fellow citizens of the planet? Are they more fools than knaves? Do they more regret the good they haven't done than rejoice in the petty advantage their sin has given them? The God who has left witness everywhere—how is God working in the Hottentot? The Christ who died for all people—how is his blood washing the stuffy diplomat, the shaven boxer, the gaunt guerilla? These questions have no irrefutable answers. The best the Spirit seems able to do is warm in us a hope that God's love penetrates even hateful situations, an instinct that all humaneness derives from the Christ. With such a hope and such an instinct, we can pray well for the coming of God's kingdom. With the Spirit molding us to realism, we will less comply with the enemy's wiles.

With some awareness of the chorus of voices shouting "madness!" let me attempt to fan these sparks into a specific fire. What might a realistic assessment of the chances for Christian peacemaking be? How might the Spirit mature a balanced conscience in the matter of nuclear arms? Perhaps struggling with these questions will make Christian conscience less esoteric, the Mystery of God both more challenging and more consoling.

When Helen Caldicott, the Australian pediatrician who has become a leader in the movement against nuclear arms and nuclear power, came to Kansas some years ago, she put together a dazzling combination of scientific knowledge, moral passion, shrewd platform rhetoric, and good luck. The scientific knowledge showed in the one-two-three way she laid out the elementary information about nuclear reactions, radiation, medical effects, and the like. The moral passion derived from her work as a pediatrician and her concerns as a mother. The rhetoric poked holes in the arguments of the advocates of nuclear power and nuclear arms. The good luck was the country's bad fortune to be going through the crisis at Three Mile Island, where we came within a stroke of a nuclear meltdown. Caldicott made no bones about her strong stand against nuclear power, and the bottom line of her case was the brute fact that we have no effective controls and can barely imagine the consequences of a meltdown or nuclear war. The best medical scenarios of a nuclear war, for example, quickly run the human fatalities into the hundreds of millions. Indeed, before long they raise the question of whether the earth itself could survive. As one fragile ecosystem, the earth is vulnerable to the gross pollution of any of its main elements: air, water, animal populations. We cannot even know how gross the pollution of nuclear war would be.[2]

Despite due allowances for Caldicott's advocacy, that bottom line remains. Thus my friend the nuclear engineer, who had long been a balanced advocate of nuclear power, admitted several years ago that since it still hasn't solved the problem of nuclear waste, the power industry is in a tight bind. No prudent person would play with such forces without much better controls. The same bottom line applies in spades to nuclear warfare. If it is even remotely possible that nuclear war would bring chaotic destruction (and surely it is quite probable), then any sane, let alone wise and loving, person of conscience would veto the means (weapons buildup) of nuclear war making. So much, then for basic guidelines, main attitudes consonant with the spirit of the Christ. What about practical political moves?

These seem to boil down to doing what one can,

accepting any compromise toward progress that intractable opponents will concede. Even when they subscribe to MAD (Mutual Assured Destruction, the theory of peace through deterrence), such opponents usually leave openings for moves to reduce stockpiles, or negotiate freezes, or increase reliance on diplomatic measures. One has to admit that in the Soviets they have an enemy both powerful and paranoid. What the MAD men and women now don't seem to see, however, is the shocking degree to which we Americans present ourselves as mirror images of the Soviets: the legacy of Vietnam, the muddied presence in Lebanon, the invasion of Grenada, the meddlings throughout Latin America. And the labyrinthine reasonings of the government spokespersons, whom we all well know cannot fully be believed, do nothing for the cogency of deterrence. Indeed, anything that does not move fingers away from nuclear triggers, reduce warheads and payloads, lessen international tensions is probably headed in the wrong direction. (I say "probably" only because the major powers' psyches are now so convoluted that one never can be sure that black won't be received as white.) Thus any political pressure in the other direction probably is a push for life.

So while people of mature Christian conscience will move cautiously, being clear that there is much they cannot calculate surely, they will nonetheless move relentlessly, trying to align policies with their clear bottom line. Anything that threatens or moves away from the bedrock proposition that nuclear power must not be unleashed has to be opposed. How it should be opposed will vary from case to case, person to person, depending upon competence, situation, and resources. But unless we can picture the Spirit enjoying the earth's moving closer to destruction, we must oppose nuclear power implacably.

## Love That Rings True

A scenario in which the Holy Spirit would acquiesce in placing the world in nuclear bondage does not ring true. Similarly, scenarios in which the Spirit would bless the gouging of the poor by the rich, the laying waste of nature, the oppression of women and people of color, and the like do not ring true. As Christian conscience matures, it grows more confident that it knows a little of what is harmonious with the Holy Spirit of love. Such a confidence is not so presumptuous as to try to speak for the Spirit. Always it must add the caveat that its discernments remain those of an unprofitable servant. But the love of God poured forth in our hearts by the Holy Spirit is a surprisingly practical touchstone. If something does not seem likely to serve, express, or advance God's love it is highly questionable. If something may be a good instrument of God's love it deserves a close look. In prayer and politics, work and sex, business and play, the love that is God's life, God's grace, is the sovereign measure. Where it flourishes we find freedom and creativity. Where it languishes we find the outskirts of hell.

So it is that prisons, death camps, gulags, torture chambers, and the like are at one and the same time godless, loveless, and hellish. So it is that self-giving love among spouses, family members, church members, and friends is a foretaste of heaven. The passion of God is the fierce love that suffers all sinful constraints.[3] The resurrection of God is the triumph of love over lovelessness, grace over sin. The mystery of sin is why creatures made for love want to resist it. The mystery of salvation is the foolishness of God, so much wiser than all human calculation, that outwits lovelessness, lures people to do good despite themselves. The Dutch religious poet Huub Oosterhuis's "Hymn for Easter Night" celebrates this divine foolishness:

> Then you did what transcends our understanding—
> on this night he was resurrected from the dead,
> on this night he disarmed and conquered death.
> He who was foolish and had no power
> to save himself became your power and wisdom.
> Your foolishness, God, is wiser than [humans]
>   and your weakness is stronger than [humans].

> How inscrutable are your ways, O God,
>     and how unfathomable is your love!
> Who was your counselor, God,
>     that you thus gave yourself to the world?[4]

It rings true to what we know of God, what the Spirit insinuates in our hearts, that God would use the ordinary, the outcast, the failing to overcome the proud and the sinful. It is consonant with God's creativity through love, healing through love, purification through love that love would be the strong man who ties up satanic lovelessness. Where satanic lovelessness cannot create, warm, or repair, Christ's spirit is always nurturing hope, warming affection, repairing frayed trust. The end of the Spirit's ministrations is what traditional religious masters have called "unitive living." This is a state in which God's presence is constant, the marriage has been consummated. Perhaps only a few especially generous people reach the Spirit's end, come before God the Judge as graduates *summa cum laude*. But even these few tell us how the Spirit is inclined, what attitudes harmonize with the divine agape. In dealings with nature, the harmonious attitudes are respectful and ecological. In dealings with other people, honesty and warmth best fit. We should handle ourselves gently and with humor. We should praise the divine Mystery always. "Though he slay me, yet will I trust in him" (Job 13:15, KJV).

On the way to such attitudes, we have to be what we presently are. So an honest anger at God is better than a pious dissimulation. Reading an errant neighbor the riot act is better than storing up resentment. Yet the justification for such self-expression is not the release of the expressor's tensions so much as the restoration of justices lost, the prosecution of loves long sought. If I shake my fist at God and never hear the equivalent of the speech from the whirlwind, I have not appropriated the full Job. Job brought his suit, made his accusations, but then submitted himself to the shifted context, where the Creator asked him for his credentials, where he had been when the universe took shape. Job's "justice" took a turn he had not anticipated, and his willingness to follow that turn was the proof of his religion. We can be what we presently are as long as we do not canonize the status quo. If the Spirit of honesty and love says jump, we should be off the cliff in a twinkling.

Does that really ring true? Is Christian conscience likely to sanction jumping off cliffs, making leaps of faith on only God's supposed say-so? Nature does not make leaps, the old sages of science used to say. The Spirit may prod leaps, ask abandonments, the old and new theologians say, because the Spirit is not nature but freedom and grace. Knowing this, loving its implications for redemption, and wanting to mature free lovers of God, Paul wrote some lines that Christian conscience can never overstudy. I can think of no better way to summarize and conclude than simply to repeat them:

> What then shall we say to this? If God is for us, who is against us? He who did not spare his own Son but gave him up for us all, will he not also give us all things with him? Who shall bring any charge against God's elect? It is God who justifies; who is to condemn? Is it Christ Jesus, who died, yes, who was raised from the dead, who is at the right hand of God, who indeed intercedes for us? Who shall separate us from the love of Christ? Shall tribulation, or distress, or persecution, or famine, or nakedness, or peril, or sword? As it is written, "For thy sake we are being killed all the day long; we are regarded as sheep to be slaughtered." No, in all these things we are more than conquerors through him who loved us. For I am sure that neither death, nor life, nor angels, nor principalities, nor things present, nor things to come, nor powers, nor height, nor depth, nor anything else in all creation, will be able to separate us from the love of God in Christ Jesus our Lord.
>
> —Romans 8:31–39

# NOTES

## Chapter 1

1. Bernard Lonergan, *Method in Theology* (New York: Herder and Herder, 1972), pp. 122–23.
2. Anne Tyler, *Dinner at the Homesick Restaurant* (New York: Berkeley Books, 1983), pp. 283–84.
3. C. G. Jung, *Memories, Dreams, Reflections* (New York: Vintage, 1963), p. 250.
4. See John Carmody, *Ecology and Religion* (Ramsey, N.J.: Paulist, 1983).
5. Mary Gordon, *The Company of Women* (New York: Random House, 1980), pp. 264–65.

## Chapter 2

1. Patrick White, *The Vivesector* (New York: Viking, 1970).
2. See Anne Tyler, *Celestial Navigation* (New York: Alfred A. Knopf, 1974).
3. See Karl Rahner, "Thomas Aquinas on the Incomprehensibility of God," *The Journal of Religion* 58/Supplement (1978), S107–25.

## Chapter 3

1. See William LaFleur, "Saigyo and the Buddhist Value of Nature," *History of Religions* 13 (1973–74), 93–128, 227–48.
2. Thomas Merton, *The Way of Chuang Tzu* (New York: New Directions, 1965), pp. 46–47.

## Chapter 4

1. See William A. Barry and William J. Connolly, *The Practice of Spiritual Direction* (New York: Seabury, 1982).
2. Alice Walker, *The Color Purple* (New York: Washington Square, 1983), pp. 177–78.
3. Rosemary Haughton, *The Passionate God* (Ramsey, N.J.: Paulist, 1981).
4. See Frederick Buechner's wonderful novel *Godric* (New York: Atheneum, 1981).

## Chapter 5

1. Eric Voegelin, *Order and History,* vol. 1 (Baton Rouge: Louisiana State University Press, 1956), p. 99.

## Chapter 6

1. See Eugene TeSelle, *Christ in Context* (Philadelphia: Fortress, 1975); Denise Lardner Carmody and John Tully Carmody, "Christology in Karl Rahner's Evolutionary World View," *Religion in Life* 49 (1980), 195–210.
2. Ignatius Loyola, *Spiritual Exercises,* no. 330, in *Obras Completas de S. Ignacio de Loyola,* ed. I. Iparraguirre (Madrid: Biblioteca de Autores Cristianos, 1963), p. 266.
3. Lewis Thomas, *The Medusa and the Snail* (New York: Viking, 1979), pp. 7–11.

## Chapter 7

1. Lucas Grollenberg, *Jesus* (Philadelphia: Westminster, 1978).
2. See Kurt Weitzmann, et al., *The Icon* (New York: Alfred A. Knopf, 1982); also Aidan Nichols, *The Art of God Incarnate* (Ramsey, N.J.: Paulist, 1980).
3. Raymond E. Brown, *The Epistles of John* (Garden City, N.Y.: Doubleday Anchor, 1982), pp. 374–75.

## Chapter 8

1. See John Carmody, *Holistic Spirituality* (Ramsey, N.J.: Paulist, 1983).

2. Lonergan, *Method in Theology*, p. 115.
3. See, for example, Annie Dillard, *Pilgrim at Tinker Creek* (New York: Harper Magazine Press, 1974); John Janovy, Jr., *Keith County Journal* (New York: St. Martin's, 1978).
4. See José Miranda, *Marx and the Bible* (Maryknoll, N.Y.: Orbis, 1974); Robert Heilbroner, *Marxism for and Against* (New York: Norton, 1980).

## Chapter 9

1. Robertson Davies, *Fifth Business* (New York: Viking, 1970), p. 191.
2. See Confucius, *Analects* 16:7; Tu Wei-ming, "The Confucian Perception of Adulthood," in *Adulthood*, ed. Erik H. Erikson (New York: Norton, 1978), pp. 113–27.
3. In addition to the famous *Small is Beautiful* (New York: Harper & Row, 1973), see also Schumacher's *A Guide for the Perplexed* (New York: Harper & Row, 1977) and his *Good Work* (New York: Harper & Row, 1979).
4. See Robert McAfee Brown, *Theology in a New Key* (Philadelphia: Westminster, 1978); John Carmody, *The Heart of the Christian Matter* (Nashville: Abingdon, 1983).

## Chapter 10

1. See John Carmody, *ReExamining Conscience* (New York: Seabury, 1982).
2. See Helen Caldicott, *Nuclear Madness* (Brookline, Mass.: Autumn Press, 1978).
3. See Haughton, *The Passionate God*.
4. Huub Oosterhuis, *Your Word is Near* (New York: Newman Press, 1968), p. 93.

# ANNOTATED BIBLIOGRAPHY

Bacik, James J. *Apologetics and the Eclipse of Mystery*. Notre Dame: University of Notre Dame Press, 1980. A good study of the primacy of mystery in living Christian consciousness.

Brown, Raymond E. *The Epistles of John*. Garden City, N.Y.: Doubleday, 1982. An exhaustive treatment of a body of literature crucial for the formation of a free Christian conscience, by the premier scholar of the Johannine literature.

Brown, Robert McAfee. *Theology in a New Key*. Philadelphia: Westminster, 1978. A good introduction to liberation theology whose themes will long outlive its bibliography.

Carmody, Denise Lardner. *Feminism and Christianity: A Two-Way Reflection*. Nashville: Abingdon, 1982. Discusses sociological, psychological, ecological, and theological issues from both a Christian and a feminist perspective.

Carmody, John. *Ecology and Religion: Toward A New Christian Theology of Nature*. Ramsey, N.J.: Paulist, 1983. A treatment of current controversies, traditional Christian doctrine, and current spiritual and ethical issues.

_______. *Holistic Spirituality*. Ramsey, N.J.: Paulist, 1983. A treatment of the major zones of life—work, recreation, health, politics, etc.—from a central focus on love.


Conn, Walter E. *Conscience: Development and Self-Transcendence*. Birmingham, Ala.: Religious Education Press, 1981. A rather weighty treatment that uses recent developmental psychology and the theology of Bernard Lonergan.

Davies, Robertson. *Fifth Business*. New York: Viking, 1970. A good novel depicting religious development over the course of a lifetime from a Jungian perspective.

Doherty, Dennis, ed. *Dimensions of Human Sexuality*. Garden City, N.Y.: Doubleday, 1979. Studies on the biblical, traditional, and contemporary theological aspects.

Dudko, Dmitrii. *Our Hope*. Crestwood, N.Y.: St. Vladimir's Seminary Press, 1977. Conversations of a Russian Orthodox priest with his people that document the Soviet oppression of Christianity.

Egan, Harvey D. *What Are They Saying About Mysticism*. Ramsey, N.J.: Paulist, 1982. A good survey of recent views about the depth-dimension of Christian faith and human life.

Ellul, Jacques. *Perspectives on Our Age*. New York: Seabury, 1981. One of faith's most trenchant critics of modern culture summarizes his life and thought.

________. *The Technological System*. New York: Continuum, 1980. A deep analysis of technology from the standpoint of a sensitivity to faith and humaneness.

Evans, Robert A., and Alice Frazer Evans. *Human Rights*. Maryknoll, N.Y.: Orbis, 1983. Case studies that dramatize the dialogue between the first and third worlds.

Fowler, James W. *Stages of Faith*. San Francisco: Harper & Row, 1981. Developmental theory applied to the unfolding of faith.

Grollenberg, Lucas. *Jesus*. Philadelphia: Westminster, 1978. A simple, lovely portrait of Jesus as a free spirit very responsible to his Father's love.

Groome, Thomas H. *Christian Religious Education*. San Francisco: Harper & Row, 1980. A somewhat heavy but liberating analysis of Christian religious education in terms of recent theological trends.

Hellwig, Monika K. *Sign of Reconciliation and Conversion*. Wilmington, Del.: Michael Glazier, 1982. A fresh look at the theology and practical implications of the sacrament of penance.

Johnston, William. *The Inner Eye of Love*. San Francisco: Harper & Row, 1978. Contemplative prayer analyzed as the unfolding of God's love.

Kegan, Robert. *The Evolving Self*. Cambridge, Mass.: Harvard University Press, 1982. Adapts the work of Jean Piaget to the stages of adult personality development—warm and insightful.

Kelsey, Morton. *Discernment*. New York: Paulist, 1978. A good, brief study of the discernment of spirits in contemporary culture, from a somewhat Jungian psychological standpoint.

Lernoux, Penny. *Cry of the People*. Garden City, N.Y.: Doubleday, 1980. A somewhat journalistic but provocative report on U.S. involvement in the repressive regimes of Latin America.

Marty, Martin E. *The Public Church*. New York: Crossroad, 1981. How evangelicals, mainline Protestants, and Roman Catholics might cooperate for the good of pluralistic America.

Nouwen, Henri. *The Genesee Diary*. Garden City, N.Y.: Doubleday Image, 1981. What a sensitive priest found when he took the concerns of his world into the silence of a trappist monastery.

Ruether, Rosemary Radford. *To Change the World*. New York: Crossroad, 1981. Christological studies aimed at criticizing prevailing cultural values and forming more authentically Christian attitudes.

Shea, John. *Stories of God*. Chicago: Thomas More, 1978. Stories of the spiritual life that make the formation of conscience the ongoing narrative.

Shinn, Roger, and Paul Abrecht, eds. *Faith and Science in An Unjust World*. Philadelphia: Fortress,

1980. Two volumes of reports on the World Council of Churches' 1979 Meeting at M.I.T. on faith, science, and the future.

Smith, McGregor. *Living Sane*. Miami: Miami-Dade Community College Foundation, 1983. A practical guide to environmental ethics.

Weitzmann, Kurt, et al. *The Icon*. New York: Alfred A. Knopf, 1982. The art of Russian and Greek devotional prayer.

Whitehead, Evelyn Eaton, and James D. Whitehead. *Christian Life Patterns*. Garden City, N.Y.: Doubleday, 1979. A good Christianization of recent reports from developmental psychologists on the adult phases of the life cycle.

# About the Author

John Carmody is a Senior Research Fellow at the University of Tulsa in Oklahoma. A theologian and writer, he received his Ph.D. degree from Stanford University in California. *Theology for the 1980s, Religion: The Great Questions,* and *How to Make It Through the Day* are among his many published works.

Dr. Carmody enjoys classical music, exercise, and contemporary literature. He has a special interest and studied background in world religions.